Praise for The Wellbeing Tc

'If you want to know how to make wellbeing part of the lived and breathed culture at your school, you need to read this book. Andrew has written a book that will empower teachers and leaders at all levels to take ownership of things that affect wellbeing. Highly recommended!'
Adrian Bethune, Primary Teacher, Author and Education Policy Lead at The Mindfulness Initiative, @AdrianBethune

'Andrew Cowley is an inspiration and a realist. *The Wellbeing Toolkit* is full of passion, strong values, principles and empowerment, and it is empirically researched, practical and accessible for all education professionals. This book should be required reading for trainee teachers, practising teachers, support staff, senior leaders, headteachers, governing bodies and trustees, stakeholders, researchers, the Department for Education and Ofsted.'
Helen Dlamini, Secondary Teacher and Leader, @Artology

'What makes *The Wellbeing Toolkit* an essential read for any school leader or school governor is Andrew's vast experience, his understanding of how schools work, and his candid, incredibly practical and viable suggestions for moving forward.'
Clare Erasmus, Head of Mental Health and Wellbeing at Brighton Hill Community School and Author of *The Mental Health and Wellbeing Handbook for Schools,* @cerasmusteach

'A fabulous read, covering such a huge amount that is utterly relevant to all those who work in school settings. Andrew has created a friendly but well-researched handbook that we can all dip into and benefit from greatly.'
Amy Harvey, Head of School, St. Peter's Junior School, @ms_jamdangory

'Andrew Cowley writes with passion, enthusiasm and the can-do attitude that is needed to help individuals and school leaders to find the confidence to take charge and create the culture needed to allow staff wellbeing to thrive.'
Victoria Hewett, Secondary Teacher, @MrsHumanities

'From principles to practice, *The Wellbeing Toolkit* is destined to make a huge impact on teacher recruitment and retention; it offers practical guidance on weaving wellbeing through the fabric of schools, for a healthier work–life balance. It's a game changer!'
Anoara Mughal, Assistant Headteacher, @anoara_a

'A practical book on wellbeing that highlights misconceptions surrounding the topic and offers practical solutions for leaders at all stages to take on board and implement.'
Maria O'Neill, Head of PSHE, eSafety Coordinator and Founder of UK Pastoral Chat, @DaringOptimist

'A great toolkit for supporting those working in schools to improve their undertaking of wellbeing.'
Rachel Orr, ITT Tutor, Education Consultant, Teacher and Mental Health First Aider, @RachelOrr

'A recommended read for school leaders seeking to retain and develop staff, transforming the sometimes ambiguous concept of "wellbeing" into practical strategies.'
Emma Sheppard, Founder of The MaternityTeacher PaternityTeacher Project, @Comment_Ed

'Andrew sets out a vision for what is possible when schools take a proactive approach to wellbeing. Packed with practical guidance and real-life examples, this book is a must-read for heads, teachers and governors alike.'
Ruth Swailes, School Improvement Advisor, Consultant and Former Headteacher, @SwailesRuth

'Seeking to help school leaders think and question practice to develop a "school culture for wellbeing to grow and thrive", this book is certainly a must-read.'
Bretta Townend-Jowitt, Primary Headteacher, @2106Head

'With *The Wellbeing Toolkit*, Andrew has written a book relevant to everyone who is invested in the wellbeing of their school. From a governor's perspective, this book offers valuable practical advice and guidance on how staff wellbeing can be made a priority. It really is a must-have resource for every school.'
Matt Young, School Governor and UK Pastoral Chat Lead, @MattGovernor

The Wellbeing Toolkit

Sustaining, supporting and enabling school staff

Andrew Cowley

Foreword by Jill Berry

BLOOMSBURY EDUCATION
LONDON OXFORD NEW YORK NEW DELHI SYDNEY

BLOOMSBURY EDUCATION
Bloomsbury Publishing Plc
50 Bedford Square, London, WC1B 3DP, UK

BLOOMSBURY, BLOOMSBURY EDUCATION and the Diana logo are trademarks of Bloomsbury Publishing Plc

First published in Great Britain 2019

A catalogue record for this book is available from the British Library

ISBN: PB: 978-1-4729-6165-5; ePDF: 978-1-4729-6164-8; ePub: 978-1-4729-6163-1

4 6 8 10 9 7 5 3 (paperback)

Typeset by Newgen KnowledgeWorks Pvt. Ltd., Chennai, India
Printed and bound in Great Britain by CPI Group (UK) Ltd, Croydon, CR0 4YY

To Zoé, Evie and Lily

Contents

Acknowledgements

This book has been a long time in the making. Not in the six months it has taken me to write it, but in the 26 years, by time of publication, that I have spent as an adult in school. *The Wellbeing Toolkit* is the result of those years of experience, of blood, sweat and tears, both literal and metaphorical. Wellbeing needs to be lived. We have all lived plenty of the tough times, and those times can make us and shape us but ultimately don't define us.

This book wouldn't have been possible without the support of some wonderful people.

Maria O'Neill, Helen Dlamini and Matt Young, my fellow founders of Healthy Toolkit who are equally dedicated to values-based wellbeing. Anoara Mughal of our team who has really emphasised the impact that values-led wellbeing can have. Maria, Helen, Matt and Anoara all took the time to proofread drafts of individual chapters, and I would like to acknowledge their input to the final text.

Cherryl Drabble and Emma Kell, both published before me, for their unwavering support for my writing and encouragement to keep going.

Chris Dyson, Monika Sandhu, Kelly Hannigan, Katy O'Connor, Hannah Wilson and Julie Hunter for their leadership of wellbeing, which has been shared on these pages.

Emma Sheppard and Charlotte Andrews at the MaternityTeacher PaternityTeacher project for their support in the gathering of material for the chapter on teachers as parents.

Sean Harford for kindly giving me his time, despite the 'Beast from the East' bearing down on Ofsted HQ at the appointed time.

At Orchard Primary School, our headteacher Jo-Anne Rowntree and all the Orchard team, who have heard me talking wellbeing and positivity, healthy lunches and values, for their patience and understanding. I would also like to thank Amanda Lavelle, the previous headteacher who appointed me her deputy, for her continued support.

This material would also not have been possible without the contribution of the 2,000 or so teachers who responded to my research investigations.

At Bloomsbury, Rachel Lindley and Helen Diamond for their support and interest in the project. A massive thank you has to go to my editor, Hannah

Marston, for having faith in the idea, persuading me to transform my concept from a 'top tips' book into the material for principled leadership of wellbeing that is in print here.

This book wouldn't have been possible either without the continued love and affection of my darling wife Zoé and my dear daughters Evie and Lily.

Foreword

What Andrew sets out to do in this book is carefully reflected in its structure.

The first section explores issues around school culture and the fundamental principles affecting wellbeing, including the importance of clear, strong values. This section encourages us to guard against adopting 'sticking-plaster' responses that fail to address the reasons for the challenges and pressures we face and to find workable, sustainable strategies for resolving or navigating them. The second section then goes on to discuss practical examples of successful wellbeing initiatives, suited to their context and with evidence of impact, together with recommended strategies, tips and hints, and useful questions for reflection. This section includes careful consideration of the Department for Education reports on reducing teacher workload and how these can be helpful, an exploration (following Andrew's interview with Sean Harford) of what Ofsted does and does not require, and the importance of career satisfaction.

So Andrew moves from principles to practice. He uses his own experience of leading wellbeing in his school to explain what can be done, and why it is so important to the ongoing good health of schools and all within them. Effective use is made of case studies to illustrate different aspects of leading staff wellbeing and what can be achieved when the vision is clearly articulated, successfully communicated and 'lived' in the day-to-day practices of the school. Andrew explores the value of a 'sideways-in' model for leading wellbeing, rather than 'top-down' or 'bottom-up', and explains that, ideally, every member of staff should be a wellbeing champion, looking out for all their colleagues in addition to the children they teach and care for.

Andrew makes use of the 2,000 online responses he received to his questions on wellbeing generally, and more specific issues such as bullying in the workplace, the pressures of balancing parenthood and challenging personal circumstances with your professional commitments, and carving out time for relaxation and refreshment in school holidays. This research helps to ensure his consideration of wellbeing is grounded in the experience of practitioners. It also underlines how building the most constructive relationships within schools and the role of leaders with respect to positive modelling, empathy, courage and setting the tone of the conversation are key.

Andrew is a realist: he accepts that teaching is a pressured profession and there will be stressful periods and difficult issues to deal with. Education professionals have to develop the resilience required to cope with this and 'self-care' is crucial. However, leading wellbeing in schools goes beyond this. Andrew explains how it requires strategic thinking, sound underlying principles, a commitment to listening and respecting the views of all the groups across the wider school community, a proactive approach to building trust and mutual respect, and a clear recognition of the reality of the work we do. What is required of those working within our schools has to be reasonable, carefully organised, sustainable and appreciated. There needs to be a sense of fairness. Collaboration can enable us to achieve more, and a focus on positive thinking and supportive, positive language can help us to find the energy we need. Communication has to be open. And all this needs to be part of the culture: the way things are done here. As Andrew says, 'Authentic wellbeing is for every day.'

This book will, most certainly, help us to achieve this.

Jill Berry

Former headteacher, now leadership consultant

Introduction

British society has been aware of a concept of 'wellbeing' since around the time of the Black Death and subsequent outbreaks of plague. The attempts by the Privy Council at preventative measures probably represent the first effort of government to act upon the health of the populace, a theme continued through the Factory Acts of the Victorian era, and the establishment first of the welfare state and then the National Health Service.

Interest in wellbeing as we might consider it now, however, dates back only to recent memory. Though wellbeing couldn't be considered a party political issue, it featured in the manifestos for the 2015 General Election (Mindfulness Foundation, 2015): by the Labour Party twice in regard to young people's mental health and wellbeing and in relation to child poverty, and by the Liberal Democrats 16 times, with a specific reference to a national wellbeing strategy. Though there was no specific mention of wellbeing in the Conservative manifesto, the then Prime Minister David Cameron had made a speech on wellbeing in November 2010, which precipitated the Office for National Statistics to begin compiling data that now forms the measures of the National Wellbeing Dashboard (Office for National Statistics, 2018). Even four years before taking the reins of power, David Cameron addressed the 2006 Google Zeitgeist Europe conference (*Guardian*, 2006), telling his audience that there was more to life than money and it was time that 'we' focussed on wellbeing, adding: 'It's about the beauty of our surroundings, the quality of our culture, and above all the strength of our relationships. Improving our society's sense of well-being is, I believe, the central political challenge of our times.' Pick through the political language, and the prominent words here are 'culture' and 'relationships', concepts at the core of schools and education across the globe. Cameron added, 'Well-being can't be measured by money or traded in markets. It can't be required by law or delivered by government.' Being an abstract concept, it cannot be, but it is from this point forward that we could say that wellbeing was firmly on our societal agenda.

Our cynical side might say that politicians make great speeches in opposition but are less effective in power and also not entirely original: Aristotle, over 2,300 years ago, spoke of *eudaimonia* or happiness as human flourishing and purpose to life. Wellbeing as a concept is therefore nothing new, but through our 21st-century eyes, where social media places issues literally at our fingertips and with increasing acknowledgement and recognition of our own and others' mental and physical health, wellbeing is becoming embedded within our vocabulary, mindset and actions, whether we promote it or not.

Why is wellbeing an issue in schools?

In its simplest terms, wellbeing is the absence of disease. Life, however, is far from simple and wellbeing is more than simply keeping well. Wellbeing in British schools in the 21st century is often ill-defined, varied, lacking clarity or lacking in its leadership, and in some cases it is non-existent.

Wellbeing for teachers and for other staff in our schools is like a multisided dice, loaded as it is with the forces brought by deadlines, time restrictions, planning, marking, monitoring, examinations and inspection. To this mix we can add the pressures of dealing with a diverse range of personalities in our colleagues, governors and parents, all this being in addition to the responsibilities to our *raison d'être*: the children in our care.

Wellbeing and workload have featured more prominently on the educational agenda in recent years, particularly in the age of social media. During the teacher union conference season each Easter, both topics reach the attention of the national press, both in print and through television. In reality though, the need to address teacher wellbeing and workload dates back to the Education Reform Act of 1988, ushering in as it did the National Curriculum, Ofsted and the age of schools being held to account through high-stakes testing.

Wellbeing itself is a broad and perhaps abstract concept. To ask any employee in education, in industry or in commerce what wellbeing 'looks like' would generate a range of diverse responses. Defining it is no less challenging: is it merely the absence of illness, the state of being comfortable and happy, or simply a general sense of confidence and vitality?

Considered within its broadest definition, staff wellbeing includes: work and workload, retention and recruitment, mental and physical health, resilience and career choice. It should therefore be of great concern to all school leaders.

We are in a time of crisis in teacher recruitment and retention. Initial teacher training (ITT) figures for 2016/17 show a decrease in new registration compared with the previous year, with only 93 per cent of places filled. Only 89 per cent of secondary training places were taken up, meaning nearly 2,000 places went unfilled. (National Education Union, 2017)

An NUT survey of leadership group members in March 2016 found that 73 per cent of school leaders, in both primary and secondary schools, were experiencing difficulties in recruiting teachers, with 42 per cent saying that the situation had got worse and a further 19 per cent much worse over the past year. Recruitment was proving a challenge in the primary sector, with 33 per cent of primary school leaders having difficulties in recruiting Key Stage 2 teachers and 23 per cent facing this same challenge with Key Stage 1 teachers. The greatest problem areas for secondary schools were in maths, science and English with 36 per cent, 34 per cent and 23 per cent of leaders reporting difficulties in recruiting teachers in these subjects respectively. (National Education Union, 2016)

In October 2016, Department for Education (DfE) figures indicated that nearly a third of teachers who joined the profession in 2010 had left teaching within five years. Of the 21,400 teachers who started working in English state schools in 2010, over 6,400 (30 per cent) had quit by 2015. DfE figures show that this trend is continuing: of the teachers who joined the profession in 2011, only 69 per cent were still teaching five years later. (Department for Education, 2017b)

To cut a long story short, we are not recruiting and retaining enough teachers. Getting wellbeing right, for teachers and for all staff, and leading wellbeing in our schools with clarity and coherence are viable solutions to these challenges.

About this book

The Wellbeing Toolkit has its roots in the Healthy Toolkit HQ blog (https://healthyteachertoolkit.wordpress.com) and Twitter account (@HealthyToolkit). Having written the blog since its inception in 2016, I realised that what began as a campaign to advocate healthier lifestyles for teachers could become a conduit for means to lead wellbeing effectively. As the Twitter account gained in following from teachers around the UK, the blog developed to cover values and principles alongside practical advice to support whole-school wellbeing. Posts about particular issues (the pressures of the long half term leading up to Christmas for example), and the responses to them, led to the realisation that many responses to wellbeing matters were reactive to events, rather than proactive in identifying matters of concern in relation to wellbeing.

The Wellbeing Toolkit aims to explore how we can lead wellbeing in our schools proactively, rather than reactively, based on a values-driven, strategic approach. The book will consider not only physical and mental wellbeing, but also matters relating to workload and career progression in the profession. It will discuss the issues of retention and recruitment by relating these to wellbeing in its broadest definition, and also reflect upon how we can lead wellbeing in a time of budgetary pressures. We hear the term 'wellbeing' quoted in the staffroom, in the education press and through teacher social media, but does this term have an unambiguous definition? For some teachers it means 'work in school and take nothing home', whereas others will take a box of marking home each evening and most weekends. In some schools, there is an expectation of availability to answer emails in the evening and over the weekend, where in others a strict 'nothing past five o'clock' rule applies.

How we address this 'balance' is not an easy matter, as all schools differ because all of our teachers and colleagues are diverse in their backgrounds, experiences, practices and mindsets. There is no 'one-size-fits-all' model of wellbeing, particularly in this era of budgetary constraint. What we do have, however, is 'culture' and 'relationships'. There are also principles, values and a commitment to making wellbeing part of the fabric of our schools. If we open our toolbox at home, among the screws, bolts, saws, hammers and Allen keys left over from flat-pack furniture ventures may be a tube of super-strength adhesive. We wouldn't glue a set of shelves to the wall, leaving our screwdriver in a pristine condition. Wellbeing cannot be addressed by liberally spreading the glue and hoping everything holds together. 'You need the right tool for the right job', as many a design and technology teacher would tell us. *The Wellbeing Toolkit* contains the right tools for the task in hand, including principles, values and the DfE reports on managing workload. As we unpack these in the subsequent chapters, we will see how schools might develop their leadership of wellbeing.

The Wellbeing Toolkit considers how we manage wellbeing for staff in our schools in its very broadest terms and how school leaders can sustain, support and enable wellbeing for all of their staff. In leading and taking responsibility for the wellbeing of our staff, we need to be aware of the state of their physical, mental and social wellbeing. This is intended as a practical publication, but also one that will encourage a reflective approach and a consideration of the values and principles that we could apply to effectively enable wellbeing in our schools.

Chapter 1 sets out to consider what wellbeing actually is and, crucially, what it isn't, and establishes my conviction that we need to have a holistic approach to wellbeing. School leaders who are serious in their commitment to wellbeing will realise that a 'sticking-plaster' approach isn't going to solve longer-term issues of retention of staff and will only make recruitment of new staff a greater challenge.

In **Chapter 2**, I will consider the principles and values that could be applied by schools in determining their approach to the effective leadership of wellbeing. Whilst no two schools will have identical statements of values, many will hold some principles in common; the schools where there is a greater understanding of what constitutes wellbeing are those where staff notice the difference.

This difference lies in the culture of the school and **Chapter 3** will therefore consider culture in detail. What I originally intended to be an optimistic chapter changed in tone as the responses by staff to the surveys I used in my research showed the extent to which the culture in many of our schools is not positive; much is quite toxic. The sources of this toxicity, alongside the manner in which it manifests itself, may come as a surprise, but I offer some proactive solutions to forestall such circumstances.

The second part of this book looks at the practical aspects of leading wellbeing, with, in **Chapter 4**, a detailed consideration of the workload reports published by the DfE in 2016 and steps some schools have made towards it. Included here are some examples from my own school, where a values-led approach to wellbeing has governed the decisions made in shaping our policies and culture. Also in this chapter is a reflection about Ofsted and workload, including the thoughts of Sean Harford. **Chapter 5** considers how we can apply our values to building good working relationships, including developing a team culture. **Chapter 6** gives time to how we might develop career satisfaction and how performance management can promote or damage wellbeing. This is followed in **Chapter 7** with a consideration of some scenarios where the culture of wellbeing and the principles held by school leaders may be tested and placed under some strain.

Placed through the book are four case studies of schools taking the time and the effort to make wellbeing a priority. Each of these schools is making a difference in their staff's experience of wellbeing. The first case study focusses on the role of the wellbeing leader. The second addresses the establishment of a new school with a sense of values, whilst the third is a school where trust needed to be rebuilt to enable values to thrive. The final case study covers the first school to receive the Wellbeing Award for Schools. With a contrast of leadership styles, of sector and of levels of deprivation, each of these schools is bonded by a shared belief in strong culture and deeply embedded values, and demonstrates a firm and authentic commitment to the principles of *The Wellbeing Toolkit*.

I am also indebted to the teachers and other school staff who responded anonymously to my online surveys both on general wellbeing matters and on more specific subjects, particularly the sections on bullying in the workplace, parental leave and wellbeing in the school holidays. In addition to these, a number of teachers responded by email or direct message on Twitter. I have protected their anonymity and left out any detail that may identify them or their workplace. Some 2,000 responses were received and these are used throughout the book to illustrate key aspects of wellbeing that are working or are challenging.

What is meant by 'principled' and 'values led' will permeate this book. Principles are crucial, because living by them and letting them determine crucial decisions are what is going to have the greatest impact upon the wellbeing of all our staff in school. At its heart then, wellbeing needs to be in the fabric of the school, in the actions of every leader and every other stakeholder. It needs to be in the culture of the school, lived and breathed by everyone, because ultimately everything we do in schools is guided by the decisions we make as leaders. These decisions impact the network of every relationship in the school.

Effective wellbeing is all about relationships and all about culture. About half of what we do in schools is about culture and relationships; the other half is about relationships and culture.

PART 1

Wellbeing, culture and relationships

1 Defining wellbeing: what it is and what it isn't

Chapter overview

This opening chapter will outline my definition of the nature of wellbeing in British schools. To describe it beyond the narrow delineation of 'the absence of illness', I will seek to clarify first what wellbeing *is not*, and then what wellbeing *is* and how it should look.

In outlining what wellbeing *isn't*, we will find:

- Wellbeing is more than mere 'kindness'.
- Wellbeing extends beyond tokenism and gimmicks and can't be covered through a tick-box approach.
- Whilst it is important to address workload, there is much more that school leaders need to consider to support wellbeing for all staff.

In thinking about what wellbeing *is*, the chapter will outline:

- That wellbeing must be part of everyday routine and practice, and it needs to be modelled, managed and led proactively.
- That wellbeing is an equal right for everyone, including senior leaders.
- That wellbeing might have a leader or coordinator, but that everyone is potentially a wellbeing leader.
- The role of the wellbeing leader, through a school case study.

What wellbeing isn't

Before we begin a discussion about what wellbeing in British schools is, it is crucial to look at what it most certainly isn't. There are many misconceptions about staff wellbeing and how it should be approached in our schools. The consequences of this range from wellbeing not being considered a serious issue that is worthy of significant attention to leaders taking a sticking-plaster approach to supporting their staff. This is not how we are going to solve the long-term challenges brought about by a lack of wellbeing. In this section, I would like to debunk some of these myths and misunderstandings, in order to help us move towards a more serious, holistic and strategic approach to staff wellbeing in schools.

Wellbeing isn't 'being nice'

In February 2017, I attended the Mayor of London's education conference, one theme of which was retention and recruitment of teachers in the capital (Mayor of London, 2017). Steve Munby OBE, CEO of the Education Development Trust, referred to retention and recruitment as one area that London schools specifically needed to focus on. Carol Campbell, Associate Professor, Ontario Institute for Studies in Education, referred specifically to the importance of people and core values, alongside leading through evidence. Campbell explained that this is how Ontario focusses upon retention and recruitment across all education sectors. The Ontario model sought to make education an attractive career, recognising that young people were more likely to wish to become teachers based on their own school experience. Mental health and wellbeing of both teachers and pupils are being addressed positively in Toronto and across the province.

During one of the workshop sessions at the conference, the opportunity arose to discuss our practices with other school leaders. Whilst some of the discussion was on the topic of London rents and the cost of living in the capital, one headteacher in our group responded to my suggestion of developing a programme of staff wellbeing with, 'Isn't that just being nice?'

In a word... no.

'Being nice' is, in short, a licence for being taken advantage of. For every teacher who begs to lose a playground duty, there will be another who wants a couple of additional days to submit reports; for the teacher behind on end-of-term tests, there will be one asking for additional support for a challenging child. Simply consenting to these requests will result in pressure moving elsewhere, either to other colleagues or more likely onto the person granting them. Schools run on deadlines, teamwork, shared responsibility and accountability, all of which are crucial elements in the wellbeing jigsaw.

'Being nice' is a short-term and *ad hoc* response to situations that should be firmly addressed in the school culture, something which I will return to in more detail in Chapter 3, page 59. 'Niceness', however, is not to be confused with empathy and genuine kindness; such values will be evident in the headteachers who are authentic in the way they lead and manage their staff. For school leaders, being ignorant of the pressures endured by our staff is no excuse. There are reasons for our colleagues to submit requests for support, and to scorn these as 'generation snowflake', a term many of us find very dismissive, raises the question of how values-led our leadership might be. This will be explored in more depth in Chapter 2, page 33.

Wellbeing isn't a tick-box exercise

Teacher social media is often an outlet for good practice, but also a sounding board for less positive experiences. Take a look particularly in early September and at the beginning of other terms when the topic of wellbeing is often raised on INSET days or in staff review meetings. In recent years, 'wellbeing can't be put in a bag' and 'wellbeing was covered in a staff meeting' were both tweeted, whilst other posts recalled wellbeing being covered on a day-long mindfulness course.

Teaching is a stressful occupation. We don't need research to tell us that. We just know it. Some pressures will be there regardless of your geographical location, intake, sector or phase; there will always be meetings, assessments, testing, marking, sickness, Christmas and so on. More recently, tighter budgets, curriculum changes, and new assessment demands and arrangements have added to the pressures upon the profession.

Wellbeing cannot be 'delivered' in a staff meeting and then forgotten about for the rest of the year. It cannot be delegated to a member of staff to deliver as part of their appraisal cycle. One course on mindfulness and ten minutes of rather awkward meditation doesn't solve anything. A bag of goodies can be a pleasant surprise, but if it is a one-off, the gesture becomes tokenistic. What use is a head massage in September to a teacher struggling to keep up with assessments in March? Wellbeing might be on the development plan but so might be extending the nursery, building a new science block or updating the first aid training.

This response to my online survey starkly enforces the point:

There has been a token wellbeing day so that they can tick a box but no sustained recognition of the need to manage wellbeing. Plus the constant pressure points don't help and no forethought to planning the calendar to support workload.'

Whilst a 'tick-box' approach might address some of the aspects of school management, such as classroom organisation, monitoring cycles or the health and safety check, it doesn't suit wellbeing because, as we will see, wellbeing isn't there to be managed; it is there to be led. Wellbeing doesn't come from a book, not even this one. Courses, blogs and tweets only effectively deliver advice and tips. A culture of wellbeing comes from your heart, not from your clipboard.

Wellbeing isn't 'massage, meditation and mindfulness'

Many of our colleagues believe in the value of mindfulness and for individuals who make the choice to embark upon a mindfulness course, the benefits for relieving anxiety, stress and mental exhaustion are considerable. Look at the popularity of apps such as Headspace, or do a search of YouTube and a multitude of self-help videos appear. Some key Twitter contacts can educate extensively about the benefits of mindfulness or of meditation. Likewise, a whole range of useful massage treatments is available: Indian head massage, deep tissue massage and sports massage to name a few. They relax, reenergise, treat cellulite and recharge the lymphatic system.

However, massage, meditation and mindfulness are ultimately about self-care. So too are exercise, healthy eating options, diet choice and 'Dry January'. Self-care is a personal choice, and although we would as school leaders always encourage our staff to look after themselves, it cannot be imposed. I have attended conferences and meetings where meditation and mindfulness have been available, but on each occasion the practitioner has always announced that if any delegates felt uncomfortable or self-conscious, they were free not to take part.

In a similar way, team-building days involving outdoor pursuits, building models from spaghetti and marshmallows or announcing something obscure that you are good at or somebody famous you have encountered or been at school with do not suit everyone. In fact they can be acutely embarrassing for some, so in this case it would act negatively against wellbeing.

In my research survey, one respondent wrote:

We have a "wellbeing group". Sometimes fruit at break, tip of the week emailed around… but I have flagged up massive workload and the impact on me personally.'

This teacher was also told, 'It's about being organised' and 'Well, that's the job, so if it's not for you…', which suggests priorities are not where they should be. Wellbeing needs to enable teachers to work in this organised manner. Is a bowl of satsumas going to help here?

The key issues with wellbeing and the wider workload agenda are far bigger than some of the more tokenistic gestures can address. Whilst there is a place for these in any school, I will argue that they will only be appreciated if the groundwork for principled wellbeing has been laid. As one secondary colleague noted:

'I think wellbeing and mindfulness are seen as a gimmick. I think by reminding us we should always put our pupils first, it is a constant guilt trip for even considering ourselves.'

This teacher further added that the revised performance measures with the new grading at GCSE increased the pressures they felt. Token gestures did little to address the real issues of workload and, whilst accountability will never be far away, an environment enabling sustained support doesn't appear to be a priority here.

Wellbeing isn't flying by the seat of the pants

Where there is an absence of strategic thinking, such as how to cover unexpected staff sickness, wellbeing can be adversely affected. If colleagues have worked in a setting where a long-term staff sickness is covered on a day-by-day basis rather than buying in supply cover for an extended period, they will understand that the impact of losing precious planning, preparation and assessment (PPA) time, scheduled SENDCo support or the additional half hour from a teaching assistant soon builds and can escalate from mild irritation to resentment. The importance of consistency and an even-handed approach to cover were common themes in my research survey feedback.

In settings with a lack of strategic thinking, the use of pressure as a strategy to organise cover emerged in my survey too, including the use of what was felt as bullying:

'I was bullied into covering lessons, doing revision sessions, agreeing with decisions I wasn't happy with.'

Sometimes in response to short-term absence, a number of replies indicated that PPA was removed at little or no notice, and in one case:

'We were denied CPD because the school couldn't be sure they could cover the lessons.'

The absence of one member of staff should never be at the cost of the professional development of a colleague.

The 'seat of the pants' strategy has also been apparent with poor organisation and communication. One teacher answering my survey regularly received emails on Saturdays and Sundays from the headteacher, asking for information for that day or the Monday morning. This suggests the headteacher wasn't organised or thoughtful enough to ask for this with a decent amount of notice. Another, in a role they subsequently left, was working over 70 hours a week. A full-time teacher was away on maternity leave, but the senior leadership team (SLT) refused to provide cover for her role and duties. Her colleague ended up over their fair share of lesson allocation and was effectively 'doing the job of 4 people'. Quite clearly in these scenarios not only did wellbeing suffer but it would appear not even to have been acknowledged.

Finally, the theme of not being thanked or recognised for taking on additional responsibilities has been a regular feature of replies to the research. In Chapter 2, page 36, we will explore the value of genuinely expressed gratitude. A token gesture of thanks is all too apparent to our colleagues when it is delivered almost as an afterthought; as one teacher observed:

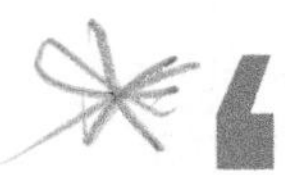

> *'It's not a few chocolates in your pigeon hole at Easter and Christmas.'*

Wellbeing isn't just dealing with workload

There were three thoughtfully produced, thoroughly considered and well-meaning reports produced in March 2016 by the DfE entitled 'Reducing teacher workload' (Department for Education, 2016a, 2016b, 2016c). Each report was written by an independent review group, and there was one on marking, another addressing planning and resources, and a third raising questions about data management, assessment and report writing. In my school, we read the work of each review group closely and with interest, and acted upon them, which is developed in Chapter 4, page 99. The membership of each group included some 'big names' from Twitter, including Sean Harford from Ofsted, and each was written in largely jargon-free and unpretentious language, making them very user friendly.

As we will discover in Chapter 4, the extent to which schools and teachers are aware of these recommendations varies extensively. As for acting upon them, this differs more widely still. The positive aspect though is that the DfE has recognised that workload is a pressing issue, has a group considering teacher workload and has run whole-day workshops to which, amongst other educational illuminati, Sean Harford and David Weston of the Teacher Development Trust have contributed.

Workload doesn't mean 'work' because the tasks our teachers do will never go away. They will still have to plan, to prepare, to teach, to mark and to assess. Classroom management and behaviour management aren't workload; they are what we do. Our teachers will remain accountable; challenging them about the progress of one child isn't workload: the manner in and the frequency at which they are asked, however, can be an example of excessive workload and does impact upon their wellbeing.

This is the key point: if you are in a challenging school, with a tight budget and little room for manoeuvre in cover, support and resourcing, you can at the very least have principles. Applying these principles to workload begins to address the wider topic of staff wellbeing, but if we recall Mr Cameron's words and consider that schools run on the fine balance of culture and relationships, then we need to bear in mind the entire experience of every member of our school community in determining what wellbeing actually is.

Wellbeing isn't a lottery

In Luke Rhinehart's *The Dice Man*, the key protagonist, bored and unfulfilled, makes life decisions on the spin of the dice. In the film *Guys and Dolls*, Sky Masterson wins a dice game having trumped an attempt to play with loaded dice. Wellbeing, on the other hand, isn't a gamble, shouldn't be down to luck and must not be loaded in favour of any interested party. Putting wellbeing into practice requires dedication and a commitment, personally and professionally, to strong core values.

Working in a team has its challenges, with a diversity of skills, ages, experiences, opinions and attitudes. Interpersonal skills, used effectively, can enable staff to forge effective relationships and work together as a team. The loaded dice, the 'spanner in the works', arises when the authentic dedication to values is undermined by the actions and attitudes of those putting self before team. This may come about as an antagonistic act, but equally likely may arise through force of personality or simply by thoughtlessness.

We need our staff to be well and both physically and mentally able to teach their classes to the best standards possible. Good leadership will guarantee PPA time, though we rarely hear it described beyond the acronym. PPA should be set in stone, but we will all know of cases, my own included in my days as a class teacher, where it has been lost and not returned. Some of us remember the days before this ten per cent of our time was theoretically guaranteed, but in the experience of our younger teachers it has become a lifeline for time out of class to reflect, catch up or get ahead. Equally, those leaders may give additional time for test marking, data entry, report writing and monitoring. Many of the recommendations in the DfE workload reviews into planning, marking and data management (mentioned on page 14) are principled and practical. It is workload that is likely to take teachers out of the profession, but factors such as support around behaviour also come into play.

In considering their own wellbeing, all staff also need to consider their colleagues. Nobody can help being ill, but the impact of even a day of absence has knock-on implications for those who have to pick up teaching responsibility in addition to other duties. Though teachers should have their release time guaranteed, some loss of it will naturally occur. Time will be paid back by good leaders without teachers having to ask for it.

The only stakeholders entitled to have a more loaded dice for their wellbeing are the children. They are entitled to the best, to be listened to as much as talked to, to have their needs met and to build the social, learning and life skills that make them the values-centred young people who will contribute to our society. Teach them well, train them well and treat them well; they will repay the care for their wellbeing by the shedload. Principled leadership of child wellbeing surely lies in a text beyond the remit of this one, but we must never lose sight of the fact that the wellbeing of children and staff are closely and inseparably related.

In rolling the wellbeing dice, we need to ensure that it can fall equally on each side. Every one of us needs to play fair and add equal weight to the care of each other and ourselves. The biggest impact on wellbeing is when individuality comes first: if we complain loudly and inappropriately or if we drain the energy of our colleagues through negative attitudes or workload contributions.

So let's keep positive and play fair!

What wellbeing is

Now we have established that wellbeing is not about using a tick-box approach to deliver gimmicks focussed purely on 'being nice' or minimising workload, let's take a look at what wellbeing *is* and how it can be led proactively and effectively for all school staff.

Wellbeing is for every day

Authentic wellbeing is for every day. The school leader with a commitment to the wellbeing of the whole staff and of all the pupils in the school sets the tone and the agenda that will enable every stakeholder to contribute their fullest to the whole school community. The message needs to come from the top, be modelled and form part of professional dialogue through the school year.

The single day of team building, massage and meditation in September isn't going to cut it when your teachers are desperately trying to meet your data deadlines in December and catching up with the children who missed assessments due to sickness, whilst at the same time juggling the demands of Christmas in the primary school. Parties, nativities and carols are wonderful for the children but for the primary school teacher this represents a time of challenge and no small measure of anxiety. Secondary colleagues are no less stressed at the end of a term that can last for as long as 16 weeks.

The school year has its 'pinch points' where pressures on individuals, departments or the whole staff are magnified; there is no escaping these points. External examinations, which are increasingly 'high stakes', will see Year 2 and Year 6 teachers and heads of maths and English in secondary schools anxiously scanning spreadsheets and gap analyses for opportunities to push their percentages. The second half of the summer term, not full of 'rounders and trips to the seaside' as some on social and in printed media might think, is probably the most pressured period of the year, especially for primary schools. With reports, sports days, leavers' productions and SATs results day, deadlines at this time of year need to be set in stone and there should be nothing, bar Ofsted and unforeseen emergencies, that comes as a surprise or requires additional work. Major changes to the timetable and the school diary need plenty of notice and time to embed; additional workload resulting from this may only cause disquiet.

Late nights at school for parent meetings, school plays and governor meetings may all be expected, but consideration needs to be given by school leaders to when these events fall. Examination dates are set externally and with plenty of notice, but there needs to be a flexible approach to other activities. Answers to my research surveys indicated some schools are planning evening events for a Friday: is this quite necessary? It is an intrusion into the weekend and into family and social time for our teachers.

One teacher told me:

> *'The staff need to feel valued so that they want to stay and teach a broad and balanced curriculum.'*

This is part and parcel of authentic wellbeing: ensuring staff feel valued and supported throughout the school year, from the first day in September right through to the last day of the summer term, enabling and motivating them to provide high-quality teaching every day.

If authentic wellbeing is for every day, then the culture of the school needs to determine this in a concrete way and the conduct of school leaders should echo this commitment. Some startling examples of wellbeing not being embedded in the fabric of the school emerged in gathering examples from teachers. Disciplinary procedures in particular are areas of concern for teachers:

> *'When disciplinary action is the focus of the start-of-year INSET given by the head, that says a lot about the school and how badly it is managed.'*

In sharing their experience of the use of disciplinary procedures in this way, this teacher has highlighted poor leadership practice. Disciplinary procedures are a last resort for teachers, bringing the school and the profession into disrepute; they are for serious breaches of codes of conduct and for safeguarding concerns. They should not be used as a stick to beat teachers with. Similarly, capability procedures should only be used in the case of a teacher for whom all other procedures to support them have proved fruitless. The procedures should be tucked away in an emergency folder. Rules and procedures are not strategies to lead any organisation with. As soon as anything is regarded as a threat, mental wellbeing will begin to be challenged. If wellbeing is genuinely for every day, then fears over career prospects and employment futures should not be present in everyday discourse.

Wellbeing is for the healthy and present as well as the sick and absent

Many colleagues will recognise having to step up when one of their number is absent for a variety of reasons because that is what we do as good professionals. We support our long-term supply staff because adapting to the ways of the school takes time. We cover duties at little or no notice. We step up because we know that somebody will do the same for us.

They should do – if the culture of the school encourages this. How we recognise, thank and acknowledge those who go the extra mile speaks volumes for the environment in which we work. If our colleagues have clearly defined parameters for how sickness will be covered, be it by supply staff or internal cover, there will be little surprise. On the other hand, reallocation and reorganisation of PPA time at little or no notice, for example, will only cause upset.

Long-term sickness provides managerial challenges for leaders. The challenge though doesn't simply end when a colleague returns to work, particularly from a mental health-related absence. However, as one teacher reported:

> *SLT were supportive when they were trying to get me back to work but [there was] no support once I was back full time.'*

I have seen teachers return from prolonged absences after hysterectomies, operations on their backs and procedures to repair injuries from their sporting pursuits. They are fully supported through risk assessment with arrangements in place for playtimes, PE lessons, and avoidance of bending down or reaching up high. Do we risk assess for our colleagues returning from a period of stress-related illness or bereavement? Do we have an understanding of anxiety or of panic attacks and the triggers that set these off? Do we make ourselves as aware as we ought to be of colleagues with autism, ASD and other 'invisible' conditions?

Wellbeing is there to be modelled

The phrase 'lip service' arose from several participants in answering my survey on how wellbeing was delivered in their setting, emphasising the point that wellbeing isn't a 'buzzword' or a tick-box exercise where it is delivered effectively.

As this example illustrates, wellbeing is something that needs to be modelled and practised, but it also needs to be enabled through a principled examination of workload.

> *Lip service is paid to the "don't work too hard" message but no solutions were given as to how to jump through hoops of our required marking and reports without working too hard!'*

'Don't work too hard' is possibly the least constructive piece of advice we could give to any teacher, because every dedicated teacher does give their utmost. Being asked not to work too hard suggests some aspects of the work can be slackened and others dropped, but which ones? This is a question that even the most battle-hardened of us could not give an affirmative answer to without very clear guidelines or effective procedures, as a further contributor notes:

> *My current school pays lip service to wellbeing but the things that they have put in place are minimal and ineffective.'*

'Minimal and ineffective', though not defined in this instance, sounds not dissimilar to the tokenistic and tick-box mentality described on page 11. If an effective and enabling wellbeing regime is going to be in place in our schools, it requires a change in culture, and this will ultimately emerge from a meaningful and principled structure.

Lip service also suggests that no actual or quantitative change can be discerned by staff. Having lived through an era of so many initiatives being introduced and teachers being told, 'You have to do this', but without effective articulation of the reasons why it had to be done, we are now surely at the point that if we make one change, we take something away in return. One observer added their thoughts on this:

> *Some small attention is paid to wellbeing but we are still getting feedback-free learning walks regularly with no focus given, graded lesson observations, increased paperwork and data drops six times a year.'*

In short, no change there.

The most impactful change that our leaders can employ in establishing wellbeing as part of their ethos is in modelling positive language in the workplace. In an ideal world we will have no negativity but of course the world is far from ideal and the very nature of our largely digital world makes negativity an easy and instant option. When this negativity begins to invade our staffrooms, we then need to be concerned for the wellbeing of our staff.

Staff may need a safe place to sound off. For some people, their wellbeing is served by the ability to have a grumble. They may not agree with every decision made by their SLT and they have the right to express this disagreement. How, when and where this is expressed comes down to a positive school ethos, allowing for constructive criticism to be given in a non-judgemental and blame-free environment. Senior leaders in such an environment will accept reasoned and polite challenge to their decisions.

If we encourage our staff to speak positively to each other, then we instantly set the tone and the ethos: we want wellbeing to be promoted and if there is to be any criticism, it is valid, polite, and non-judgemental, and will not undermine the mental wellbeing of our colleagues. Negativity is a drain. Repetitive and constant negativity will undermine confidence. As Adrian Bethune (2018) tells us in *Wellbeing in the Primary Classroom*, for every negative interaction with a child, there should be at least eight positive ones. Why don't we repeat the same balance with our colleagues?

Wellbeing is an Ofsted concern

In researching this book, I interviewed Sean Harford, National Director of Ofsted. A fuller evaluation of our discussion can be found in Chapter 4, page 113. We discussed at length how some aspects of past inspection frameworks had been misinterpreted and had become ingrained in the thinking of some schools. The principle case in point was the expectation of 'progress in 20 minutes', which emerged in the early to middle part of this decade and which was near impossible to measure and infrequently delivered on a meaningful basis beyond a 'staged' lesson. Yet somehow the '20-minute rule' became embedded into expectations of a lesson observation, most likely because that was the amount of time we might expect the inspectors to stay in the room.

Sean has had a few bruising encounters on Twitter, which, given the nature of the medium and of his position, he would come to expect. However, the myths that have 'polluted' the thinking of our system go back further than the time Sean and Amanda Spielman were in post. The 'myths' that have been weaved into the lexicon of the 21st-century teacher and that challenge our notion of teacher wellbeing are embedded in the taking as gospel of initiatives such as these:

- A 'carousel' of activities in the National Literacy Strategy – a suggestion, never a rule.
- 'Numeracy' and 'Literacy' being lessons that had to take an hour.
- 'Assessing Pupil Progress' grids, which some schools were still using even as levels were being eliminated.

A little history lesson perhaps, but for the primary sector it was these initiatives, and those that followed, which began to tip the balance of paperwork and workload into more challenging territory.

'Myths' impact on everyday notions of wellbeing, where headteachers and advisers or consultants use the vocabulary of 'what Ofsted want'. Ofsted inspect our schools; they don't run them and as public servants they are subject to scrutiny as much as any other inspectorate. Ultimately, Ofsted impacts us for a couple of days every two to four years depending upon your judgement, longer if you have another result. Accountability is part of our role as educators, but it should never be used to wear down the wellbeing of our teachers.

Wellbeing is about the 'bigger picture'

Although wellbeing management has naturally focussed in no small part on teacher workload, which will be covered in Chapter 4, page 99, approaches to the topic need to take a more holistic approach. If we think solely about workload then we consider only our teaching staff, yet the most successful schools consider the whole range of their employees.

We need to consider also more than the core of planning, marking, data management and assessment. For example, do our behaviour policies promote wellbeing? If they do, our staff can feel assured that they will be supported in times of difficulty and that they can be confident of the backing of school leaders. On the other hand, shoddily worded and inconsistently applied policies raise questions, sow doubts and undermine confidence, which in turn can impact on mental wellbeing.

Attention needs to be paid to the ethos and atmosphere of the staffroom too. Ideally it is a welcoming escape from the rigours of the school day, but it can be a hotbed of dissent and dissatisfaction and a sounding board for the malcontent. Equally it can be a space dominated by a vocal minority, a clique or the person who always wants to be heard – the 'staffroom mouth' as one respondent named them. Are our staffrooms genuinely social areas or do we have some staff who never venture beyond their pigeonhole?

If wellbeing is for every day, this includes every moment of every day. This means not encroaching upon our colleagues' evenings and weekends and especially not their holidays. We need to consider the whole range of emotions and life experiences that all of our staff live through: pregnancy and parenthood (for both parents), the challenges of raising children, divorce, bereavement, debt, anxiety and stress, illness, success and failure.

Remember, we need to live and breathe wellbeing to truly embed it in our school culture.

Wellbeing is for everyone: do you know your staff?

We have established the principle that wellbeing is for every day, but of equal weight is another principle: that wellbeing is for everyone and everyone has an equal right to it, with no favouritism and no exceptions. If the authentic right to wellbeing is established as a universal and egalitarian principle, it is for senior leaders to take the reins, to set the example, to model the good practice and to make clear their expectations. In being proactive, leaders need to know their staff.

Knowing your staff is akin to knowing your pupils. A knowledge of the children's data alone means that the teacher knows the numbers but does not necessarily have an effective teacher–pupil relationship. As class teachers, the knowledge of a child's background, behaviours, triggers and interests is what builds this relationship.

In the same way, do we really know our staff? For every individual who shares every detail of their life with their colleagues, there will be another of whom we know little. Do you as a school leader know the names of your colleagues' partners or children, where they went for their last holiday or their choices in food, cinema or reading material? Or maybe your only conversations are around planning, progress and attainment, in which case a rather soulless working environment would result. Do you recognise who may be vulnerable to different pressures, who doesn't enjoy the staffroom banter, who has things going on in their lives that add other burdens to their load? SLT need to listen and to talk. We need to be able to differentiate between personal and professional dialogue and staffroom chatter.

Wellbeing days and the activities they feature are not for everyone. Whilst many a senior leader would retort with 'We're a team', we need to be fully aware of the sensibilities, vulnerabilities and tastes of our colleagues. The same applies to a truer application of wellbeing principles. Some teachers can flag up quickly if they are in difficulty and in need of support, whilst others will keep their concerns to themselves. Within this group there will be those who know they have problems and find it uncomfortable to admit it; equally there will be others who are unable to recognise that they have any issues.

Yet each and every one of them has the same right to wellbeing as their colleagues. Where staff have moved from one school to another, they have realised this:

> *I've worked in schools where wellbeing of staff wasn't a priority and it showed in absence, low morale and a bullying/cliquey culture of blame.'*

Moving school after several years of living this experience made this colleague realise it wasn't normal, and a weight was lifted as they moved on.

Everyone may be different but the obligation to look out for all our staff needs to be built into SLT expectations. Several replies made mention of wellbeing raised in end-of-half-term review meetings, begging the question about what happened in the previous six weeks or so. A more specific commentary added:

> *The leadership team "appear" to have wellbeing as a whole-school priority, but in practice nothing has changed. It's a show for Ofsted, to pretend they're doing something. Our last "wellbeing" staff meeting was spent being told off for not wearing hi-vis jackets when outside on duty and being reminded about staff absence procedures.'*

Spot the wellbeing there. In leading wellbeing, bringing a 'management' concern into the arena, alongside a perception of negativity and criticism, is actually going to undermine confidence. The likelihood here is that the concerns may have related to one or two staff. In the same way as we wouldn't tell off a whole class because of the poor behaviour of an individual or small group, the same should apply to dealing with staff. In my experience, in the days when we had six weeks to prepare for Ofsted, we were all called in at lunchtime just as we wanted to be prepping our classes for the visit the next working day to be harangued for 40 minutes because one person hadn't completed their register properly. The anxiety in the room was palpable.

Happily, some more supportive environments were reported in the survey, including the following two examples. In the first, the SLT take great care to ensure that their staff are healthy. They have daily debriefing sessions and monthly one-to-one sessions, to talk through any concerns but also just to give them the opportunity to talk, and support is always freely available. In the second school, the management of wellbeing is described as 'extremely subtle', with some wellbeing initiatives in place, but the focus of the SLT is on reduced scrutiny, fewer, more reasonable and less burdensome expectations from policies, more PPA time and minimal micromanagement.

Wellbeing is for SLT too

A strong theme from the leaders who responded to my research was that in some cases their wellbeing wasn't being considered by their staff, governors or trustees. It really is important to remember that our senior leaders are human too and in many cases have been in class until recently or still are on a regular basis. Heads and deputies will, in the interests of the school, 'bookend' the day, handle a lot of flak and other incidents that never reach the classroom. It should also be remembered that senior leaders have the often emotionally draining and time-consuming responsibilities related to safeguarding. Anyone who has remained at school until ten o'clock at night awaiting completion of activities by social services or the police will appreciate these sentiments. SLT do need to be 'battle hardened' and know how and when to protect their staff and children but are equally as entitled to their wellbeing as everyone else in the school.

Wellbeing is best led 'sideways-in'

A 'top-down' model of wellbeing is not ideal because wellbeing is not 'done to' our colleagues but is part of the process of working with them. 'Bottom-up' similarly does not capture the essence of what wellbeing should be, implying as it does subliminal messages about hierarchy and entitlement; it doesn't suit an egalitarian image of addressing the topic. The intended model that I have introduced in my school is 'sideways-in', which embraces 'ownership' of wellbeing. If wellbeing becomes part of our professional and regular conversation then ideally it can be spoken of openly and not hidden in a corner.

Led purely by senior leaders, the danger is of wellbeing becoming simply part of 'management speak'. In the analysis of responses to my surveys, I found teachers and other staff often wore their hearts on their sleeves. However, in my surveys specifically for school leaders, there were some considered replies to the question 'How do you promote a culture in which wellbeing can thrive?'

One school leader emphasised the open-door policy of their SLT, meaning their availability to listen and talk. Staff were granted an additional ten per cent of PPA time and the directed time budget was planned to allow for staff to have contact with parents. The ethos of school policy allowed staff to take care of their wellbeing. The SLT included both the senior mental health leader and staff wellbeing leader. Some very careful budgeting is apparent here, which is not a luxury available to small schools on tight budgets and perhaps not as sustainable as school bank accounts continue to shrink.

A model that some cash-strapped schools could follow comes from this example from a secondary school leader. In their school, there are no whole-school marking expectations and departments are left free to do what works, including the use of whole-class feedback and doing without written reports. Staff aren't expected to cover for absent colleagues and no interventions are planned for the holiday periods.

Another school leader reported that most decisions in their school are made after consultations with staff, which is clearly not a 'top-down' system of leadership. Staff all contribute to decisions about what initiatives are implemented or otherwise and, if new workload is introduced, something else is taken away. The most effective thing was the updated marking policy, enabling marking to be mostly done within the lesson and for the benefit of the children rather than for any scrutiny. This respondent added that staff were given plenty of non-contact time to fulfil middle leadership and subject leadership roles effectively and that they had a strong team spirit.

Common themes in my leadership survey in regard to wellbeing included aiming to provide a supportive environment and for leadership to be approachable. Many leaders emphasised their willingness to listen and to encourage a work–life balance, as well as to ensure a degree of personal support. Many others recognised that improved communication between staff and senior leaders was a wellbeing priority.

One headteacher, however, responded to the question of how they enabled a thriving wellbeing culture with blunt honesty:

> *'I don't. The staff will all leave anyway if they don't like it.'*

This negative attitude towards engaging staff in the wellbeing process is repeated elsewhere, as another contributor identified that there was an attitude of 'if you can't stand the heat', adding that they had witnessed SLT and middle leaders almost bullying a teacher for a lack of behaviour management skills in the form of an action plan, with no care for their wellbeing at all. Another reported that in a previous school there was a culture of bullying 'from the top' and an expectation of work and availability day and night, including weekends. This teacher was asked, 'How do you expect to do the job if you are not prepared to put in the hours?' In both these cases the teachers made the choice to leave their schools and continue their careers elsewhere. The culture they left behind, however, remained.

Some schools have allocated the leadership of wellbeing to a middle leader or another member of the staff team, or to a wellbeing group. A number of responses considered this to be a positive step, giving ownership to the class teachers and teaching assistants, rather than the school management. This does require senior leaders to ensure that such a position is well managed and the person in role taken seriously. One school, for example, had a class teacher as wellbeing coordinator. SLT didn't listen to their input and their role was little more than someone who led icebreakers at the start of every term and organised the Christmas social. There is no acknowledgement here of what a wellbeing regime should genuinely consist of. In another institution, the SLT had set up a wellbeing group. However, with the lack of a defined role and clear outcomes, this group wanted to focus on staff socials rather than the experience of late nights, meetings and workload that teachers faced on top of the burden of travel between two sites. By way of contrast, one headteacher gave the role of wellbeing leader to one of the middle leaders, but the position was taken to mean 'wellbeing spokesperson'. Every initiative and change that the SLT tried to implement was met with, 'The staff don't like this and you need to think of their wellbeing', even though this may have been the opinion of just one or two and not of the majority. This headteacher added, '[The wellbeing lead] is a blocker and I despair at my decision.'

How each individual school goes about setting the scene for wellbeing depends upon a range of factors, but in each of these examples we are witnessing the failure of the school culture to engage all parties effectively. The wellbeing coordinator reduced to team-building games during staff INSET isn't engaged effectively in the task, as leadership patently aren't supporting the role. Depending upon your standpoint, the wellbeing leader using wellbeing as a lever to block what the head regards as desirable change may have a genuine desire to protect the staff, but they may also be hindering school development. Wellbeing is not about blocking change; wellbeing embraces change where change is for the mental, physical and social good of every stakeholder.

The role of the wellbeing leader

To whom do we give this role? On page 26, I identified that in some schools the role was given to somebody outside SLT with the result that their role became little more than social secretary or alternately one that was a 'blocker' to change. However, a positive and enthusiastic wellbeing leader can set an example that places the care for wellbeing firmly on the agenda, as this case study outlines.

Case study: The proactive wellbeing leader

Monika Sandhu

Monika Sandhu is a wellbeing leader in a secondary school in the home counties. She has held various posts in different schools, all within pastoral and academic roles. Monika is Assistant Headteacher and Curriculum Leader of Science in her current school, and she has an outstanding record of recruitment and retention as well as exceptional results each year. Monika is a firm believer in 'Teamwork makes the dream work', and her staff are her most valuable resource. She has worked hard to create a climate of trust, through taking risks and empowering staff, where growth and development are at the forefront. The impact of this has resulted in year-on-year exceptional outcomes for both staff and students, and staff wellbeing has been at the heart of her department.

As an acting assistant headteacher, Monika started to introduce whole-school wellbeing during the examination period, the busiest and most stressful time of the year for staff. She introduced 'Wellness Wednesdays' for all teaching and non-teaching staff. There was a different focus for each of the first six weeks:

1. Health benefits of drinking lemon water; staff were provided with lemons.
2. Ways to recharge, such as meditation, walking appreciation breaks and stretching.

3. Healthy eating; staff were provided with fruit as part of their five a day.
4. Health benefits of sleeping well and ways to sleep well.
5. Connecting with each other, family and friends; staff were given noughts and crosses, hangman and make a square games.
6. Mindfulness of the breath; staff experienced a mindful cup of tea or coffee.

This was very successful and staff felt valued and cared for. After initial positive feedback, Wellness Wednesdays continued into the next term where they utilised 'secret staff talents'. A new member of staff was able to offer military fitness, another was certificated in meditation, and one was a talented Bollywood dancer. Every Wednesday after school, staff chose to go to military fitness, meditation, Bollywood dance classes or simply home to spend time with family and friends. This was extremely powerful, as it brought so many members of staff together who maybe had not spent much time with each other or did not know each other. Do you know how talented your staff are? You will be pleasantly surprised!

Throughout the years, Monika's school has invested in staff wellbeing, and now the following initiatives are embedded within the wellbeing offer:

- directed time for data inputting
- voluntary workshops
- free tea, coffee, milk and sugar
- Christmas end-of-year celebration
- summer end-of-year celebration
- reporting made simpler: no staff comments, only dropdown boxes
- a computer-based data programme to sort data into specific groups
- admin team consisting of five members of staff
- non-teaching pastoral team consisting of six members of staff
- lunch for INSET days
- food to sustain staff on parents' evening
- free use of fitness suite.

The school wanted to build upon the wellbeing work Monika had introduced as acting assistant headteacher, and she was successful in securing the permanent role of assistant headteacher, which includes responsibility for staff development and wellbeing.

Education is facing some challenging times with both continuous educational changes as well as difficulties in recruitment and retention. Even though the school started focussing on wellbeing, it was decided to make staff wellbeing a school priority, so one INSET day the school was brave and bold by asking staff for their voice. The school has listened to the staff and has promised to deliver.

In response to the staff survey, Monika will putting in place a range of measures, including:

- regular staff voice meetings
- introducing mindfulness
- the kindness envelope challenge, paying kindness forward
- directed wellbeing time including a range of activities
- social committee
- specific monthly wellbeing focus
- flu jabs
- five-minute wellbeing plans
- lemon and ginger tea during the cold season
- reverse advent calendars
- staff Christmas celebration
- Dry January: staff are given smoothie shots to sample, weekly recipes and fitness classes
- sleep hygiene 'top tips'
- sleep music
- Wednesday curry and chat
- examination period survival kits
- hydrated water flavours, lemons, oranges, limes and blueberries provided for four weeks during the examination period
- steps challenge in teams for the summer term
- a wellbeing board to promote healthy lifestyles and choices

- mindfulness sessions in place of morning briefings
- quick wins throughout the year to relieve stress and anxiety.

What next? There is still so much that can be done, such as having a staff relaxation and de-stress room, a wellbeing committee to continue to drive staff wellbeing, as well as mirroring wellbeing with the sixth form students and then eventually with all students within the school.

Monika has a real passion for wellbeing and believes wellbeing is a lifelong journey for everyone, and as schools we need to be brave and always find time to notice our staff, connect with them and look after their health.

We need to make wellbeing count if it is going to make a genuine difference to the daily working lives of our school staff. As you read the subsequent case studies in the following chapters, you will see further examples of what effective leaders of wellbeing are putting in place in their schools: authentic, values-led wellbeing that makes a difference to the staff and has a direct impact upon the children. If your wellbeing leader isn't on the SLT, it is important that they have a voice and that their voice is respected and listened to by senior leaders, otherwise the role may simply be washed away as they become the person who organises social events and Secret Santa. If your wellbeing coordinator is one of your leaders then they need to speak with an awareness of budget realities but also with a passion and authority on the subject of the wellbeing of all of the staff. Don't forget the small stuff: everyone should be a wellbeing leader. Wellbeing ultimately is about people, their lives and their emotions.

Toolkit takeaways

As a school you need to reach your own definition of what wellbeing is because each school is different. Wellbeing in a small village primary school is going to look very different from wellbeing in a large urban comprehensive. In many ways, however, they will be similar, because in leading and managing wellbeing you are dealing with people and each school's wellbeing journey is going to be mapped by the relationships within that school.

Wellbeing isn't about being nice; it is often about hard and sometimes harsh decisions. In setting out your strategies for wellbeing, some starting points and high expectations (a preferable term to 'non-negotiables') will set your journey in the right direction:

- Choose your wellbeing leader with care and ensure they have the full support of SLT. It is essential that they have had some positive and negative experiences on their own wellbeing journey. Nothing gives you better knowledge of the need for wellbeing than a few tough times. The headteacher is not the best choice for the wellbeing leader but maybe you have an enthusiastic, passionate and eloquent school leader to lead the agenda.
- Embed the positive language of wellbeing into your conversations; establish the habit to drip feed it into your school culture.
- Make the key decisions that will set parameters: how absence will be covered, when the deadlines are going to be, what notice of major changes will be given and so on. Stick to these with total consistency.
- By all means offer massage, meditation and mindfulness, but don't restrict your offer to this and the occasional cake or bowl of fruit, otherwise you will be seen as delivering a token.
- Challenge myths, especially 'Ofsted want to see this' because usually they don't.
- Know your staff, know their strengths, know their triggers and know their anxieties.
- Look after your own wellbeing. SLT deserve it too. Set the example in your conduct and expectations.
- Be consistent, visibly consistent.

P.P.A. is very stressful for Valence staff - space, computers that work, nearby refreshments

2 Essential and effective wellbeing values

Chapter overview

This chapter outlines what I regard to be the key values that school leaders should employ in their wellbeing strategy. These values are the tools in a school leader's wellbeing toolkit and need to be authentic and deeply held. We will consider practical means of working with and delivering each value.

We will consider how we might support the values of:

- celebration
- collaboration
- respect
- trust
- support
- perseverance and resilience
- courage
- empathy
- time.

There is no 'one-size-fits-all' model for wellbeing, and every wellbeing toolkit will differ for each school. Just as each DIY toolkit has its common elements of saw, hammer and screwdriver, the commonality of principles allied to the values in this chapter can provide the basis of your wellbeing toolkit, to which you can add the screws, nails and glue.

Those readers familiar with the work of Jane and Neil Hawkes will recognise the principles and philosophy behind values-based education. Even if you aren't, values will often be written into school mission statements and their mottos. Ultimately they should be felt within the ethos of the establishment. Of the leaders who, in responding to my survey, gave me their thoughts about how they managed and led wellbeing, many, as we might expect, agreed that their leadership style was highly governed by a valued and principled approach. The nature of the platform on which my questions were raised and the content of the survey may beg the question about how representative these answers are of the whole of the leadership of British schools, but for those answering the survey, with a commitment to at least discussing wellbeing, this was most encouraging.

In a values-led school, pupil wellbeing is enhanced by them understanding the impact of their words and actions upon others and their relationships. The same values should, where used consistently, also apply to professional relationships among staff. The strength of those relationships will ultimately determine the wellbeing ethos in the school. The values outlined in this chapter can form the basis of a strategy for a school that makes the mental and physical wellbeing of all stakeholders an absolute priority.

When we founded the Healthy Toolkit HQ blog and Twitter account as a platform to discuss and promote wellbeing, in our mission statement we determined that our thoughts, words and actions would be guided by the values that we held dear in our personal, pedagogical and leadership experience. We are all shaped by our experiences. Every one of us has experienced joy, grief, excitement and disappointment. We have been let down or supported, embarrassed or praised, lied to or even lied about. Heartbreak, romance, childbirth, promotion and pride, all of these impact on our thought processes, self-awareness and life decisions, and make us the people that we are.

Some values are universal; others are personal. People with diametrically opposed views will still contend that they have strong values that determine their line of thought. Values will often be determined by socio-economic context, cultural factors and the strength of sense of community. When we introduced values-based education in my school, the values cycle that we chose as a whole staff was determined by the context of the school, whilst also recognising that there was universality to our chosen principles.

In looking after our staff, and by extension our children, what values can school leaders hold dear in determining how mental and physical wellbeing is going to be promoted and prioritised? How do we choose a principled approach, embedding and practising our core values, which guide our personal and professional behaviours and which determine our fundamental beliefs and thought processes?

Contexts will vary for each leader. The village primary school with two or three classes and the inner city academy with 2,000 pupils over two sites or more couldn't be more different. Pressures may be in stark contrast even in schools within the same community, as staff experience and availability vary considerably. There are, however, some core values that, with a lateral rather than linear philosophy, apply broadly across the contexts of all British schools. We will consider each in turn and explore how they can be applied in the workplace.

Celebration

What do you do well? Plenty! But do you realise this? Do we thank each other enough? Are we positive in our mindsets? Do we notice what others do? Celebration of children's achievements is an underlying principle of a successful school, but at the heart of that school is a team of adults striving to deliver the positive future our children deserve. It takes seconds to thank somebody, praise their efforts or a particular piece of work and if this is sincere, rather than a token, the value for the recipient is immeasurable.

The core of celebrating our achievements lies in its authenticity. Read any informed guide to behaviour management and it will tell you that children will soon see through some strategies, such as the child who is non-compliant for four days of the week but knows that by 'playing the game' on Friday the class reward is for their benefit too and maybe some individual recognition will come their way as well. Likewise the children who always do the right thing but may not be the 'high flyers' of the class may go almost unnoticed; they are the 'Invisible Children', as James Pye (1989) termed them. Now ask the class to speak openly about their feelings on this topic and many will tell you it isn't fair that those who behave impeccably, complete all their class tasks and homework and show exemplary manners receive fewer rewards than their less committed peers.

Apply these thoughts now to your staff. Good leaders know and trust their colleagues to fulfil their role to the best of their ability but inevitably, and this is the case in other areas of public service too as well as in commerce and industry, some will go the extra mile, give '110 per cent' and stay beyond their contracted times (a good teaching assistant or member of office staff is 'gold dust') or (in the case of teachers) give more than their commitment to their class and their subject.

How do we acknowledge this? Clearly not in the way that one teacher described. This teacher's first head could never say 'thank you', not one to one and certainly not in front of staff. The head would also return end-of-year reports in the early morning briefings, making a point about grammatical errors and spelling for all to hear. In the year the teacher left, they were determined not to make a single error. When the reports were handed over there was one with a sticky note on top. The omission was one comma, out of a total of some 45,000 words. The teacher recalled, '"There are some changes to make," [the head] said in front of everyone. No thank you, no acknowledgement of the effort. What a b******!'

When I write the weekly staff newsletter, there is a section at the top left always reserved for thanking staff and I am determined that it is genuine. I always try to ensure that everyone gets a regular mention and it acknowledges those who go 'above and beyond', supporting PTA events, covering in an emergency, taking the initiative and the like. Yet it also acknowledges taking classes on trips, running sporting events, leading cultural pursuits and organising class assemblies. Following these up with a personal email, WhatsApp message or written note, thanking them for the day-to-day tasks that often go unnoticed can have a profound impact.

We mark the children's achievements, certainly in the primary sector, with weekly celebration assemblies, visits to the headteacher or deputy head, stickers for exceptional work and messages home on the class rewards app or at the gate at home time. Never underestimate the value of a shiny sticker; it is the source of great pride for children. Do we celebrate the achievement of our colleagues enough though? The cynically minded might suggest that we shouldn't thank or praise people simply for doing their job, but teaching isn't any ordinary job. Well done to all the accountants, insurance sales staff and call centre operators, but they don't have the emotions, the relationships, the highs and lows, the hours or the frustrations we do. I suspect only the staff in our health service would be able to empathise with the teaching profession.

In my school we mark each 'zero' birthday with a personalised cake and Prosecco – if appropriate. I know of some headteachers who mark every staff member's birthday with a card and cake or flowers. Small steps, insignificant perhaps on their own, but in the 'big picture' these represent parts of the wellbeing jigsaw.

Celebrating and praising is a tricky one to get right. We don't want to appear like a gushingly overzealous children's television presenter nor as an awkward Alan Partridge-style character with words that are either embarrassing or meaningless. Public praise isn't for everyone either, and if you were giving someone attention at the end of September, for example, a point not at the end of a half term where the bog-standard thanks are given, you might get the 'What about me?' comments from some colleagues and who would blame them? Authentic leadership won't make a public show of an individual, but will recognise the small things that make a difference; 'I noticed how much Sam's writing has improved. That was a really well-crafted piece I saw on display' takes seconds to say and is evidence of your 'visibility' as a leader.

Gratitude and recognition need to be genuine. The thanks on the weekly newsletter need not be just for the trips and sports fixtures but also for stepping up for playground duties or first aid – the small, seemingly insignificant events that help the school tick over. Recognising each of these shows leadership awareness and the consistent drip effect of honest appreciation will be valued in return.

Collaboration

Look at the most successful teams and the most surprising teams. Leicester City became Premier League champions in 2016 because they played to each other's strengths. There were players who received greater attention than others but the attention of all was to the greater good of the team. The 'spine' of any successful football team is at the root of a winning mentality: the core of goalkeeper, central defender, midfield and centre forward is largely unchanged over a century and a half of tactics. Balance, as Sir Alex Ferguson (2016) points out in his book *Leading*, is the key. The rest of the team sheet can't be filled with spare goalkeepers and third-choice defenders. The balance doesn't simply occur once then remain constant. It requires perpetual work, fine-tuning and awareness of the developing strengths and frailties of those in the organisation.

The same model could be applied to the management and leadership of a school, but whereas Sir Alex conducted a 'fire sale' of players to move on elsewhere, this principle cannot be applied to schools. To any new headteacher inheriting an established staff, the challenges must be daunting, particularly following on from a lengthy and successful regime. Inherit a positive culture and mindset; don't rock the boat; let things run as before: all these things are much easier said than done and any governing body appointing a new head will consider change alongside continuity. To persist with the football analogy a little longer, when Brian Clough inherited Don Revie's dominant Leeds United in 1974, 44 days of unmitigated disaster ensued, yet his next appointment at Nottingham Forest cemented his reputation and legacy.

A new headteacher will inevitably seek to make an impact, either with a sense of immediacy or over a longer and more sustained model. The core staff who have remained after the departure of the previous incumbent are imperative to continued success. Having said this though, more than one respondent to my research reported a new headteacher making clear that they had a 'hit list' of staff to be removed, which is a concern as a direct threat to their wellbeing and does not fulfil the value of collaboration.

Collaboration needs to work both ways, however, as a headteacher new in post discovered when experiencing what they defined as bullying by staff 'set in their ways' and determined to stand up to the new face. They told the headteacher that they could not use the staffroom and held union meetings about proposed changes during the school day. They used their influence in the community to make life difficult and unpleasant. The headteacher recalled, 'My union rep told me later that he'd thought from what they had said that I was a complete monster.'

In my first year as deputy head, I kept on a whiteboard in my office a tally of 'favours' I had asked of the teaching assistants and support staff, of lunch duties, emergency cover, supporting in the office on census day and a myriad of other tasks. Intended only for my own reference and sense of fairness, it was soon noticed. The impact of it came when one teaching assistant who had grumbled about how much extra they were asked to do was marched into my office by their colleague to the words, 'See! He's being fair!'

Wellbeing needs this sense of fairness in working together. The unpredictable nature of school and the multitude of interactions, reactions and behaviours each day are going to leave us needing to ask somebody to step in to help. The 'it's not my job' line is commonplace in workplaces where a sense of frustration about fairness sets in. Don't expect the teacher who regularly loses PPA time or is asked to give up their teaching assistant for the day yet again to be too cooperative. Given the squeeze on budgets, sickness absence or attendance on courses is going to mean more is going to be asked of our colleagues. The wellbeing challenge is to be fair and not to leave the sacrifice to any one person. Keep a tally of your requests, keep it fair and equal, and be prepared to show it.

When a school is under strain, be it from tight budgets, a series of absences, tension in parental relationships, worse-than-expected results or an impending inspection, teamwork may be put under some pressure. This in turn can have a domino effect on staff wellbeing and the potential is there for a cycle of anxiety and failure. Negativity is draining and needs no help in gaining a foothold. Our challenge is to challenge negativity at every opportunity.

It need not be this way and indeed matters often reach this stage because of overthinking. A year of poor results can be reversed the next year; parental relationships can be sorted with an open-door policy and greater availability; Ofsted – it's two days every few years (through gritted teeth). My point is a little simple psychology can avoid the overthinking and turn negativity into positivity. In a one-form-entry primary school, one child is worth 3.3 per cent of the data; parents with an issue aren't monsters – they just want to be heard; an inspection, whatever the outcome, can be thought of as a positive experience – even a challenging inspection can be regarded as an opportunity to make positive and impactful changes in policy, practice and attitudes. To take another analogy from the sporting world, it is like the fear of the penalty shoot-out. The England team had succeeded once in a shoot-out before 2018. Let's face it, whether a fan or not, we all expected failure on each occasion. The overthinking of the penalty and the whole shoot-out competition put the pressure on the next taker. As we know, Gareth Southgate's England buried that pressure and lived with one missed penalty against Colombia in the 2018 World Cup. Think the same with your team at school. Past 'failures', negative mindsets, *'these parents'* and *'these children'* need to be put aside in changing how we think. Good wellbeing can grow from effective team spirit in positions of seeming adversity.

As we will explore further in Chapter 3, page 59, school cultures and relationships are delicate yet crucial parts of the wellbeing jigsaw. I will argue that successful schools have a culture of collaboration at the hub of their operation. Even the mavericks and the individualists might subscribe to this ethos.

Respect

As a frequently misused term in 21st-century society, respect should be a value that everybody has for each other, but in an era of instant criticism through digital media, unpredictable political behaviours and socio-economic tensions, it is one that may appear absent. Self-respect can regulate our own words and actions. In our team we have mutual respect for the range of each other's talents and skills. We respect each other's opinions and discuss any differences openly, fairly and without prejudice. Any effective team has the same moral code as its foundation.

If we are to deliver wellbeing effectively across our school, by implication respect needs to be embedded and be equally applied regardless of role and responsibility. As we all know, however, respect is something that has to be earned and cannot be instantly expected, as any NQT who challenges the difficult parent in the first week of September has found to their detriment. Likewise, the new headteacher, without the personal charm and manner of the previous incumbent, will find out the very same thing when building relationships with parents, children, staff and governors.

Respect doesn't come from fear. I recall from my PGCE in the pre-internet, pre-digital age (1992 – don't judge me) the head in my first practice school proudly announcing to the four of us, 'Half the staff left when they knew I was coming'; it was hardly a ringing endorsement for their leadership with potential employees for the year to come. One teacher in a primary school told me that their old headteacher, retiring after 25 years and 'the loveliest man you could meet,' invited the new head for a tour in early June, but instead of the handshakes and small talk routine that might have been expected, the occasion felt like an Ofsted inspection: 'We were all on the back foot from September and staff had left classes and the office over the first two terms as the fear factor multiplied.' In this school the head stood down eventually, reportedly under some pressure, but in many other cases reported to me new headteachers have overseen a near 100 per cent overhaul of staff within a year of taking post. Building respect in any establishment will take time, patience and no small amount of emotional intelligence. Leaders ultimately set the tone for a school, but one where the staff fear for their positions on a whim of an observation or a caustic comment is not an institution where teachers will remain for long.

Fairness builds naturally into respect. There is an obvious hierarchy in schools but everyone relies on each other in the smooth running of the school. 'I don't do cups!' one of our cleaners told me on my first day as deputy head, and why should she? She has enough to do and, as she frequently points out, the teachers couldn't do their jobs without her fulfilling her duties. Leaving a set of dirty coffee cups in the sink, leaving that pen lid by the bin instead of picking it up, or walking past the discarded milk carton in the corridor and expecting someone else to deal with it – all of this is both lazy and implies a lack of respect. Wellbeing dictates that we have a healthy respect and recognition for all of our colleagues.

Visible and consistent respect from headteachers and other senior leaders sets the tone. An 'us and them' mentality, or an aloof attitude to other staff, creates resentment and is divisive. These are your colleagues, not your personal assistants. Job titles and salaries aside, these people are your equals. Do you take your turn making the break-time tea or leading the shared lunch? Are you in the corridors on parents' evenings doing a tea run for your parched colleagues or in your office and out of sight? Do you still take your turn in the classroom?

One of the most visually striking examples of respect, and a statement of the school ethos, can come from the simplest source: the staff photograph board in the lobby or reception. The traditional presentation is one of headteacher followed by SLT, teachers and support staff. This will leave some people at the bottom and sends a subliminal message of who is in charge and of a clear hierarchy. Your colleagues pass this every day on the way into school and it is a reminder of structure. Some, however, imply through their arrangement the sense of equality your culture may wish to embrace. A circular or alphabetical arrangement sends a very different message to the 'family tree' model. For added impact, try dropping the job titles. If you want a real leveller, cast off the posed photographs and ask the children to draw each member of staff.

Is this addressing wellbeing issues? Remember, we are addressing wellbeing as a holistic issue. By building visible respect into our school culture, we communicate that this is our expectation and that everything else builds from it, and we put the wellbeing of our colleagues firmly on the agenda.

Trust

As a school and as colleagues we come together as strangers, but mutual trust in each other's underlying beliefs and abilities should build and strengthen our teams. What happens, however, when this trust is missing? The very best schools and businesses run with trust at the nucleus of their operations without everyone being monitored and appraised to extremes. Without trust, personal and professional relationships are at risk. Trust means that someone is there for you when you need them, can maintain a confidence and take on responsibilities.

Whilst gathering the material for this book in 2018, we had another change of Secretary of State and after some consideration of workload and the pressures of inspection, he announced to the NAHT Annual Conference new principles for a clear and simple accountability system, in which he proclaimed that he trusted schools and leaders 'to get on with the jobs', which by implication suggests that a level of trust may have been absent at Department level. Whilst this book doesn't address issues of government policy and expectation, the cascade effect from the decisions of our elected leaders and appointed officials inevitably ripples into schools with the pressures of high-stakes accountability. As Damian Hinds said, the 'spectre of our accountability system can loom large over schools' and 'Fear of inspection. Fear of a single set of bad results. Fear of being forcibly turned into an academy – all of this can create stress and anxiety, and that can percolate through the staff.' (Whittaker, 2018)

As we will see in the next chapter, the erosion or non-existence of trust is an essential element in disrupting the positive culture of a school. Teachers who for years have turned out excellent results through high-quality teaching do not need to be required to jump through hoops merely to tick a box somewhere. A primary school teacher who teaches mathematics to a high standard does not need to be observed time and again teaching mathematics. Unless there is of course another agenda: to ensnare them on a 'bad day', to prove some perceived level of professional standards, to put pressure on, where it may never have been before, or to catch them out for some other purpose.

Trust is also eroded in regimes where teachers are expected to show something that they have been proven competent upon years ago. Planning is perhaps the best example here. To a 'good' teacher, planning is second nature; resourcing, differentiating and meeting the range of need are embedded in their practice. Yet when we hear of such teachers receiving negative feedback for 'not planning your differentiated questions in response to the pupils' lack of understanding of the concept', this begs the question of the level of trust held in them. In teaching, many eventualities cannot be planned for, but teacher intuition, resourcefulness and subject knowledge ensure that learning gaps are filled.

Where trust is lacking, teacher wellbeing will suffer as we look over shoulders, become defensive and maybe adopt strategies to avoid the net of criticism. School leaders trusting their staff to deliver, and those using monitoring cycles as an effective 'sound check' rather than a trap, will inevitably have that trust repaid in a multitude of other ways.

It is difficult to imagine any school working effectively without trust between all the members of staff. Micromanagement implies that there is little or no level of trust and the manifestation of the micromanagement impacts wellbeing in a variety of ways. Overzealous monitoring, the weekly check-up of plans and the unannounced book looks with no feedback put teachers on edge and eat into the weekends and evenings as they ensure they are up to date. Micromanagement relying on 'telling tales' erodes trust between colleagues, and can be seen as a divisive action in a strict hierarchy of responsibility. There is a difference between mentioning a genuine concern and trying to get someone in trouble, which can be evidence of workplace bullying.

This isn't a question of individual trust; it is organisational trust that is breaking down when the culture permits such conduct. Where trust is absent or not visible, this is where wellbeing is going to be under strain, triggering anxiety attacks and staff taking time off with stress. The strongest teams, whether we use a sporting or a workplace metaphor, rely on high levels of trust, interdependent working and a shared authority, which a micromanaged establishment won't have. Trust takes time to build and can only do so through positive relationships and sustained engagement through whatever management structure is in place. The ever-shifting goalposts of standards and expectations will not enable a trusting infrastructure to develop. Build the trust and the wellbeing will flourish with it.

Support

An organisation with an established level of trust will match that with the level of support within it. If we continue to take the 'sideways-in' model of wellbeing leadership, as established in Chapter 1, page 24, this can mirror our support structure. The greatest support needs to come from senior leadership. This needs to be visible and multi-directional; it is not a matter for the person in need of it to come in search of it, but for leaders to know when to offer it and for colleagues, in the atmosphere of trust, to know when to alert leaders to the need of another.

Are we open enough to admit when we need support? Probably not, although we all need it, whatever our level of responsibility at school. The best schools will keep an eye out for children and staff who are struggling, need a leg up or need some time to reflect or manage their time or their emotions. Even the very best at managing their own time will slip up on occasion.

How often though is the first reaction to a mistake, an omission or a failure to complete a task by a deadline one of criticism or an assault on one's abilities? Do we stand by our colleagues as we would our friends in times of trouble? Do your school staff stand as one and know they have the backing of each other? Or would they not think twice about stabbing one another in the back?

In developing a school culture where teachers and other staff are trusted and where wellbeing will thrive, the culture needs to be supportive and inevitably the example needs to be driven from the top. Where the school leadership is openly critical of individuals or groups, there will be an atmosphere either of fear or of resentment generated. Such open criticism can emerge where there is public criticism of teachers in staff meetings, in corridors or in the staffroom over lunch – all have been mentioned. On other occasions, conversations are overheard where doors have remained open or where voices can be heard through walls.

If we have a values-led school, then the whole staff need to believe in the values. Cultivating a supportive environment means challenging the perceived negativity of some members of staff and digging deeper to uncover the reasons for this. A case study, to be found in Chapter 3, page 69, will show how one headteacher did just this in a challenging environment.

Support means more than having a poster on the wall with telephone numbers and websites to contact. If a member of staff is having a crisis, personally or professionally, it shouldn't be a matter of shoving a card in their hand but a situation requiring a personal touch. Talk, listen, and show a level of understanding. We won't know all the answers, but the human side, the empathy that we show, demonstrates the values we live by. By all means share the work of organisations such as the Education Support Partnership and local support such as counselling services, but please talk about it rather than point your finger at the poster.

Talking is important in the value of support. That is why under the Healthy Toolkit banner we launched our 'Tea and Talk' initiative, which promotes effective conversation in school that goes beyond the confines of education. The tea element is not mere alliteration; to make and to enjoy a 'proper brew' requires time and that time allows for discussion to develop. Easy to set up, it could be hosted by a head, SLT, governors, teachers or teaching assistants, and it could be one-to-one or support a small group. It could last all year, be every term, every month or every week. Essentially this is time set aside for talking and listening – not *talking at* but *talking to* – and promoting wellbeing and healthy attitudes. There is increasing stress placed on teachers and support staff. If we are seriously going to address the worries and issues of our professionals, a channel to voice their concerns to colleagues is vital.

Gone should be the critically negative language of monitoring or an observation. 'You didn't do this…' can be better phrased as 'Perhaps you can try this…' but more importantly in feeding back findings to other leaders, instead of identifying the weakness as a means of isolating or pushing a teacher out, the positively minded leader will see an opportunity for growth. A support programme shouldn't be a means of levering out but one of helping someone grow, because to have a concern about their career and job security is going to have an adverse effect on their mental wellbeing. We can all think of colleagues who have found times hard in one school and been put on a support programme to move them on, but in redeploying elsewhere have flourished where trust, respect and support are in place for them.

Positive language makes the difference. The 'positivity feedback sandwich' may be a little clichéd, but having consoled someone after a negative response to the words of another, we can appreciate that there are different ways of sharing areas for development rather than bluntly listing points for improvement.

If SLT have been trained in coaching techniques, the language used in feedback may become more affirmative. Open questioning, such as 'How did you feel that went today?', as opposed to the closed 'Was that a good lesson?' allows for more of a dialogue to take place, which, in establishing that perhaps the learning wasn't as great as it could be, is more shrewd and probing than a forthright language choice might be. Reversing statements into questions will still have the same effect but will allow for greater reflection and ownership of what might not have gone well. Positive language isn't a matter of being polite. Used well it can still have the impact that a critical tone can have but without the same negative bearing on the mental wellbeing of the teacher.

Making the language positive at all times is a challenge. It takes leaders who can craft a sentence carefully to reinforce the culture, values and ethos of the school through the trickiest of times. I am sure we have all had the experience of working with someone with all the subtlety of typing with caps lock left on and have winced in response. Consistent and authentic thanks, feedback, greetings and interactions – all are at the heart of the leader who makes the support of their staff the highest priority.

Perseverance and resilience

To turn to mindsets and growth mindsets in particular, to persist in a task, to search solutions, and to accept failure but learn from it are all features of human behaviour through history, from sparking the first flame to landing on the Moon. As we have discussed already, there is no instant solution to the issue of wellbeing in school, but the development of a series of strategies, trialling them and evaluating them with an open mind represents a way forward. Failure need not be feared but should be built upon and learned from. Is your philosophy one of endurance and being there for the long haul?

There are few occasions when a change in school is going to have an immediate and visible effect. In discussion of changes to behaviour policy, Paul Dix (2017) suggests that it takes at least 30 days for any change to be visible and perceived. With any initiative that is going to positively impact wellbeing and workload, this is going to take much longer to be visible – maybe a term, possibly a year. This is because in changing the culture of a school, considering the holistic nature of wellbeing as well as shifting workload patterns, it will take the entire cycle of a year to appreciate them.

At the end of a long, hot summer term with pressures such as a tough Ofsted inspection, end-of-year reports and data collections, not to mention hay fever, insect bites, staff departures and arrivals, our resilience is often tested and stretched. This test of resilience is also a test of the school culture. How does your school maintain and reward the value of resilience? By pulling down the blinds and hoping it goes away or embracing the issue full on? Wellbeing doesn't stop because term is nearly over. The toolkit needs to be open and ready to be used at any time.

'Get over it! It's in the past now!' is probably the least helpful advice in motivating staff whatever the workplace. What these words, or some variation on them, represent is a lack of awareness of context. Imagine if this had been used in a conversation between two colleagues. The difference of impact on a teacher between, on one hand, the key stage leader having a word because of a poorly mounted display or, on the other, a parent shouting abuse is immense. Getting over the first can be done with a quick fix; the second can potentially end a career. Lessons can be learned from each scenario, but for a newly qualified teacher being on the receiving end of a parental tongue lashing in their first week in post is going to challenge resilience from the outset.

In building a good team culture, and particularly in growing a resilient attitude, there is much we can learn from the world of sporting achievement. Pete Sampras was top of the world rankings for 286 weeks, won 14 Grand Slam titles and only lost four finals. He was not unpopular, but he was never acclaimed in the same way as Cash, Agassi, Nadal or Federer. Sampras betrayed little emotion, even in victory. He wasn't a man for climbing the stands, jumping the net or throwing his racket in the air. Yet before each final he was unable to sleep, paced his room and was wracked by nerves. Come two o'clock though he was in control, in the zone and able to shut out the crowd, the noise and his opponent.

Our teachers face a Grand Slam final every day not just in front of their classes but with every challenging child, difficult parent and computer glitch. Keeping the level of detached cool that Sampras showed is no mean challenge, but a skill that leaders learn, perhaps after a few harsh lessons themselves, but it is one worth passing on. I have led a meeting supporting a less experienced colleague with a challenging child or parent on many occasions. Maintaining a level of 'detached cool' means shutting out negative thoughts. The choice of language used by the school staff needs to be consistent and calm, even though with a child there will be the cheeky and challenging behaviour that can be a defence mechanism, and from parents a few expletives can be expected. Put aside the 'I won't be talked to like that' attitude for a moment and consider two things: schools are about relationships and some people will articulate their argument this way – don't judge them. The implication for our staff wellbeing here is that modelling the calm and fair approach, which restorative practices and the use of a micro-script would support, minimises the stress that our adults might feel. Micro-scripts are pre-prepared conversations, often listed on cards, with a short sequence of statements to use in addressing or defusing behaviour situations. 'How do you keep that calm?' I was asked once by a colleague who had to challenge a difficult 11-year-old. I had to reply in the moment that I didn't really know, but reflecting upon that occasion, it comes down to consistency and, as far as my colleague is concerned, offering 100 per cent support to them.

Courage

We have the courage of our convictions. We stand by each other, stand for each other and stand up for what we believe in. We face up to criticism and answer it with all of our core values at the heart of every decision, response and action. Seeking an easy life and pursuing the comfortable option isn't always available. Holding steadfast to our principles drives our beliefs and the programme we wish to develop and deliver. How brave are you as a school leader to do this? Do you give into demands for an easy life? Delegate tough tasks and confrontational situations to others?

The most courageous leaders are those who are consistent, visible and trusted. They do not have to be loud; they need not broadcast every decision from the rooftops. They do however have to make some decisions that are tough, especially when it comes to wellbeing. We need to make hard decisions, but decisions based on the reality of the situations we manage because in addressing wellbeing, one of the strategies in our toolkit is making the challenging choices that benefit the majority rather than appease the vocal minority. Wellbeing is ultimately about people, the relationships between them and how those relationships impact on the way they perform.

Brave decisions can be made in regard to marking policies or planning requirements, for example, in the face of comments like 'Traditionally we have always done this' or 'Well, this gets us our results', which are often thrown as a shield to any changes. Change does bring an element of fear in any workplace and I believe particularly in the minds of our more recently qualified teachers, used to, as they are, the rigid confines of a range of centrally driven initiatives: the literacy and numeracy strategies (if they trained in the late 1990s); the demands of the 'new' curriculum; the disappearance of levels for Key Stage 1 and 2 assessments; and the appearance of Progress 8 measures for our secondary colleagues. Change brings fear. Changing demands may be one factor behind long-term retention issues. Fear of change impacts the wellbeing of our staff and it takes courageous leaders to make, lead and manage the change that our schools need while at the same time looking after their staff.

It takes courage to stand up and challenge the voices that resist, insist or believe the myths. A case in point: the school leaders who come back from meetings with statements such as 'Ofsted want this' when, in many cases, it isn't in the inspection framework and inspectors don't want to see this. In my experience as English lead, there were many occasions when a colleague returned from a course on one of the many initiatives that peppered the first decade of this century convinced that we were 'doing everything wrong' and that we had to change. More recently I took issue with an external adviser who insisted that my colleagues should be doing six data drops a year. Quoting my insistence on wellbeing first, the workload reports and the tweets of Sean Harford, I held my ground.

Do you have the courage to challenge in this way? Do you put your colleagues first in the face of such demands? Do the meetings and courses described in the last paragraph encourage debate and questioning, or is the audience there as a sponge to absorb every word as if it is gospel? We will explore some themes relating to leading and managing change further in Chapter 4, page 99.

One of the bravest decisions for a leader to make is how to acknowledge and act upon the actions of someone who is adversely affecting the wellbeing of others in the school, because to do so clearly spells out a commitment to a positive culture. Among the issues raised in my research surveys, these were the broad categories that teachers and other school staff expressed their concerns about:

- workplace bullying, often by long-serving and influential members of staff
- marginalisation and social exclusion around the school, in the staffroom and at social events
- gender-based and racist language and discrimination
- speaking unprofessionally to and about others
- picking up the consequences of a colleague with poor behaviour management strategies or unwillingness to follow policy
- mismanagement of a long-term sickness, resulting in greater workload and disproportionate loss of statutory PPA release.

In most of these circumstances, the general sentiment was that people 'got away with it' in the cases of the way they spoke to others or of bullying. Reasons cited were favouritism, fear of conflict or fear of the consequences if a certain person was challenged.

Favouritism, actual or perceived, can undermine self-confidence and give the feeling that whatever you do isn't good enough, especially when compared to others. Favouritism can also fuel rumour, as we will see in Chapter 3, page 59, and if this gossip falls into the hands of a person with influence on younger, less experienced or more susceptible colleagues, this can spiral.

The 'fear factor' is a tougher equation to crack. In schools with a toxic culture, one or more staff, individually or in a cabal, can act as if they are immune to authority or are overt in their challenge to the headteacher and other leaders, particularly when the leadership has been recently installed. The perception that someone has been given into or allowed to have their own way because they shout loud enough or win allies to their cause due to their influence can alienate the quieter members of staff, but also impact their mental wellbeing with a feeling that there is an aspect of being treated unfairly. It is very telling when the seemingly 'fireproof' people remain but the 'new blood' of staff leave in frustration.

In the case of someone's performance not being up to scratch, there needs to be a balance between their wellbeing and that of the teachers affected. It takes

a while to bring a class back to focus if they have had lesser expectations for half a day, especially if required to revisit learning with them, which negates the impact of preparation time. The other teacher might be having issues focussing, personally or professionally. It is easy for people to be judgemental without knowing the actions you are taking. Formal and informal support plans should be confidential. I am afraid a few very direct 'this is not your business to ask' conversations need to be had here.

Nobody, however, should be in fear of their career, as it is job security that is at the root of much mental anguish for teachers. If somebody isn't performing to standard and is not responding to a support plan, then encouraging them to move on, for their sake as well as their colleagues, is the best option. Likewise with those involved in cliques and favouritism, they still have bills to pay. Unless there is a serious breach of teachers' standards, nobody should fear for their job.

It takes a brave headteacher to make a stand, perhaps through one of those fierce conversations but also by being blunt in public about a high level of expectations to support teacher wellbeing. There needs to be no excuses in regard to any aspect of staff wellbeing. Burying one's head in the sand when it comes to bullying, cliques or preferential behaviour solves nothing. Giving a clear statement of intent makes quite transparent that your message to the majority is that their wellbeing is your priority.

Empathy

ITT courses cover the essentials of being a teacher in class, but do they prepare our new teachers for the professional elements of their role, such as the way to conduct oneself with colleagues, senior leaders or parents? Leadership courses likewise cover leadership styles, holding staff to account and planning for change. Neither overtly addresses a core value that we try to instil in our young learners: empathy.

A school with wellbeing at its heart needs to have an empathetic approach from its leaders. Though we have already discussed wellbeing not being a top-down approach, leaders who are both visible and visibly empathetic can model the attitude for their staff to work to.

Empathy is the ability to experience and relate to the thoughts, emotions, or experience of others. Empathy is more than sympathy, which is being able to understand and support others with compassion or sensitivity. Some people are naturally empathetic; others lack empathy totally; whilst the majority would fall into a category of being somewhat or sometimes empathetic. Empathy can be learned, but it takes coaching and practice to embed this attitude into the mindset of leaders. As part of the wellbeing toolkit, empathy is an invaluable device. Ultimately it is concerned with listening and being aware of the needs, emotions and experiences of your staff. Be wary though not to fall into one of these categories:

- The leader who can't listen. This sort of person won't have the time to meet; the need to listen arguably needs to be fairly immediate. This leader will delegate the responsibility to somebody else who may only give feedback in the form of a diluted summary of the issues, which benefits neither party.
- The leader who won't listen. These leaders tend to be those who respond with 'if you can't stand the heat', 'the grass isn't greener elsewhere' or 'it's part of the job' in response to wellbeing, workload or behavioural concerns. Empathy is absent here, as is any obvious care for mental wellbeing.
- The leader who can only listen. They will typically nod the head, offer a supportive shoulder in a meeting but when the need for action arises, nothing concrete is put in place.
- The leader who doesn't listen. They are good at offering solutions but forget that the person they address isn't like them, works differently and has a dissimilar experience from themselves. These solutions will be 'talked at' the recipient rather than talked through. Behaviour management strategies and classroom organisation are two issues that many a new teacher may discuss; however the strategies of the experienced but perhaps more traditional teacher are not always going to suit somebody just coming to terms with running a class for the first time. When it comes to coping with the pressures of parenthood and balancing school work with family life, advice from someone without their own children or who didn't take the same level of responsibility with their own children is, truth be told, no advice.

The leader who listens and acts is in effect the mentor or the coach who facilitates the change that might be required for the individual concerned. The change may be something minor, such as popping into class once or twice a day or giving a reassuring word about an aspect of work causing anxiety, or may involve a shift in organisation to address a more pressing concern. Such actions demonstrate the visible empathy that shows how each member of the team is valued.

Another aspect of empathy is the ability to say 'thank you' and crucially to mean it. We have all received empty thanks, hollow platitudes or even been unacknowledged for our contributions to success over time. One teacher in my research survey reported that their headteacher said, each year, 'I can only reward hard work with more hard work' and that the words 'thank you' never passed their lips that anyone could recall.

Meaningful thanks don't come in the form of a banner, cakes or even in a deserved day in lieu. Consider the impact of a personal email or text, a written message or even the spoken word. Genuine appreciation, with the reason outlined and expressed with feeling, can lift the spirits. Thanks issued with honest and authentic warmth and meaning make a difference and can promote a sense of belonging and teamwork. Don't throw around the thanks out of a sense of conscience and please make sure that everyone is included.

Empathy has two elements: acknowledging an issue and the reaction to it. We acknowledged on page 49 that empathy isn't really covered in ITT or leadership training. Empathy, like wellbeing, is not about 'being nice' to people. To address empathy in a team, we need to think less in a linear way but in a more lateral manner.

Both primary and secondary colleagues will be familiar with R. J. Palacio's *Wonder* (2013) and its maxim of 'choose kind', which has formed the basis of many a PSHE lesson. Yet how many schools that encourage their pupils to 'choose kind' have the same in their interpersonal relationships with the adults?

The first step to empathetic acknowledgement is to ask and to be open. A starting point is a wellbeing survey but these need to be written and executed carefully. Long answers are time consuming and could potentially compromise confidentiality if the content or style is identifiable. A scoring scale is a better tool, with 'agree', 'disagree' and 'neither' as a minimum set of options. The wellbeing survey may not give the answers you want to hear, and a good deal of leadership resilience to a few harsh answers is required. Being prepared to listen and to act is important and it's essential to build these into an action plan. Budgetary realities mean that some of the expectations staff may have are going to be a challenge to deliver, but the crucial element for the wellbeing leader is to show that you have listened to concerns and are willing to address them. Don't forget though that wellbeing is for every day. One survey in September isn't the only time we need to talk about wellbeing. Having an open door and an open ear to concerns your staff have will be noticed. Acting upon those concerns evidences your empathy. Give it time, particularly as a new leader, but if you are prepared to listen and to take action, then you develop trust as well as build empathy.

Empathy though cannot be carried by one person alone because eventually it will drain them. Empathy that is genuinely compassionate comes from the team culture that we build, so the logical step is to build empathetic behaviours into staff training: appropriate behaviours, trusting relationships and developing authentic understanding. It is our young teachers who we need to target here as they are our headteachers of the future. The breadth of your wellbeing strategy can be used to bring our latest generation of teachers in touch with genuinely empathetic skills. With these they can all become wellbeing leaders.

Empathy is difficult to teach but it can be modelled. The first aspect to exhibit is staying power. This isn't simply revisiting resilience, but modelling the longevity that seems to be required to keep our young teachers in the profession. The rower Dame Katherine Grainger is an example of the spirit of staying power we would wish to encourage our youngest teachers to have. Time after time she came up short in the Olympics, silver, by her high standards, not being good enough, though in the glorious experience of London 2012 she delivered the gold medal her dedication deserved. Another rower, Sir Steve Redgrave, went through pain, diabetes and semi-retirement to win a fifth Olympic gold medal. If we are going to have the Graingers and Redgraves in our schools, we need to build the necessary resilience in our teachers' wellbeing through our empathy with them.

The second aspect to build into our empathy kit relates to speed of thought and can again be seen in sport. For every sharp catch in the slips or impeccably timed run and volley into the top corner, there will be a mistimed passing shot or long misplaced pass into acres of the wrong space. Quick reactions can turn a result; it is the equivalent quick reactions that enable us to diffuse the trickiest situations in our classrooms and in conflicts between children or between parents. Whilst our sporting stars can be entirely intuitive in their match-winning moments, it is the skill of the senior leader to make their action seem so. In fact, the quick thinking in dealing with an argument between parents is often the result of years of experience, just as in truth it is in sport. Here is where we need to be proactive: stand with your teachers at the end of the day and be seen to respond to situations that may arise. Support your teachers in those initial tricky meetings with parents or challenging children. This visibly demonstrates your empathy for them, and shows that their wellbeing is your priority and that you can give them workable strategies for the future.

This level of empathy requires us to support and work alongside our young teachers in particular if we wish to keep them in the profession and develop their leadership capacity. With our longer-serving staff too, there are lessons to be learned if we are going to make everyone leaders of wellbeing.

Time

Granted, time isn't a value. It is a resource, the most precious resource your teachers have, and although there isn't going to be a magic bag of time in your toolkit, what we can do as school leaders is protect it and not fill it with meaningless tasks and meetings.

Anyone who has sat through an interminable staff meeting, particularly at the end of the summer term, will appreciate the cost of wasted time. One primary school teacher reported in my research survey a meeting on the last Monday of July lasting three hours, having the diary for the next term read to them, day by day even though every member of staff had one in front of them. It was riddled with mistakes and not cross-referenced to the equally error-laden timetable. This was followed by a haranguing of the staff, despite excellent SATs results, for the 'failure' to plan 'properly' and a string of minor misdemeanours. The staff left the building at half past six demoralised and browbeaten, without a word of thanks for their efforts.

Though this length of meeting is a little extreme, many teachers reported meetings regularly exceeding the agreed limit and often drifting off agenda. One subject lead reported that the training session they had planned meticulously was pushed back by a lengthy 45-minute discussion on the staff night out. A common sense approach would have been to use the 'any other business' part of the meeting for this. Instead, teachers had little professional benefit from this INSET, as the meeting exceeded its designated time and attention drifted elsewhere.

PPA time has had several mentions in the text already but it is ten per cent of our time that has become invaluable. It needs protecting and guaranteeing, not taken away at very short notice and certainly not carried over to another week. For some teachers, especially those with a young family, their weekend wellbeing relies upon the efficient and uninterrupted use of their non-contact time. It is a statutory requirement and one that should be efficiently planned for. The long-term sickness of one member of staff, as a number of teachers have told me, should not be used as a reason to change the cover at short notice.

We need to respect the individual units of time that our teachers have and also need to think about planning ahead for time. The 'pinch points' in a school year come thick and fast and some weeks offer more stress than others. It is a thoughtless head who timetables a data drop in the same week as the Key Stage 1 nativity, or who throws in arbitrary deadlines as the end of term approaches and time is running low.

Time is the most difficult resource to give, and the easiest one to waste. Waste your own and you penalise only yourself, but waste your colleagues' time and nobody will forgive you. Long and tedious meetings with no meaningful outcome, tasks that only create additional work with no benefit to learners or teachers, and events with little or no notice only go to erode goodwill and question the level of trust and respect in a school.

* Our staff verbalise frequently - Why have Monday briefing that often repeats Friday AT bulletin.

Give your colleagues the time they deserve and the time they have earned. Respect and support their time, celebrate it and trust them to use it, have the courage to protect it, empathise when it is wasted and repay it when you can. Time is precious. Time and the staff we employ are our most precious resources. Have complete respect for and trust in both, and your wellbeing toolkit is being put to the best possible use.

Case study: The values-led school

Aureus School and Aureus Primary School, Didcot

Hannah Wilson is known to many school leaders through Twitter and in particular for being a co-founder of #WomenEd. Hannah had the opportunity to build a school culture from scratch when appointed as the founding headteacher of Aureus School in Didcot, Oxfordshire, part of the GLF multi-academy trust (MAT).

Having nearly a year to establish and build the concept and values that she envisioned, with the characteristic energy those who know her from #WomenEd will attest to, Hannah set about her mission of 'nurturing hearts and minds' by selecting a dedicated team to open the school in September 2017.

Look at the student prospectus and written large is 'our wellbeing culture' and a belief in 'a holistic education to develop the whole student'. The environment is very clearly one in which the development of each pupil, socially and emotionally as well as academically, is the clear priority. Deputy headteacher Julie Hunter is responsible for wellbeing and culture; how clear a commitment to both is it possible to have?

Wellbeing at Aureus starts with the children. Each morning, four days a week, begins with a session of mindfulness. These are not exercises in simple meditation; the biology and neuroscience of the practice of mindfulness are at the core of each pupil's education. There is also a very clear programme to talk about mental health and to discuss issues such as depression in an appropriate and non-judgemental manner. Prevention and intervention are at the root of good mental health and wellbeing education. Aureus was also able to offer The Didcot Art Room, who were going to be homeless, a base in the newly constructed building and their community art therapy sits at the heart of the school. While not every pupil engages in the wellbeing process, the strategies are there for them when needed.

Good wellbeing for pupils is rooted in sound wellbeing for staff. The Aureus staffroom is labelled the staff wellbeing room. No internal phone line, no staff mobiles, and an absence of computers and of educational books and periodicals gives a clear message that this is a place for the staff to come to relax. As a new build, this is easier to prioritise, but how many other staff spaces are as dedicated as this? I have seen many staffrooms where there is not sufficient space for everyone and that double up as PPA rooms, resource areas, secure storage spaces or even group work areas.

Within the first year of opening, Aureus attained the 'Values Quality Mark' from Neil Hawkes' values-based education group. The core values of the school – diversity, equality, wellbeing, responsibility, respect, kindness, love, empathy, courage, confidence, integrity and resilience – underpin all the decisions made in the school. These values and the resilience that Hannah wished to embed in her school, which her Twitter followers had seen growing in the 12 months before the first Year 7s rolled in, are clear to see. The school embodies its values through its curriculum and its culture and the whole staff embraces them.

As Aureus began its second year, where other schools had cut therapeutic services, they invested in a 'Thrive Room' with two trained thrive practitioners with two more in training. They created a 'Nurture Room' and have recruited a dedicated nurture team to deliver what Dr Neil and Jane Hawkes call the 'Inner Curriculum'. With their sibling, Aureus Primary School, which opened in 2018, they are striving to show that there is a different way.

Moving forward

You may have little in the way of financial flexibility but you can have principles because principles cost nothing. If, as leaders, we take a principled approach, if we have our guarantees of what will and what will not happen in our school, we clearly demonstrate the commitment to a culture of wellbeing. By having the courage to speak up for and to represent what is right, if you are empathetic and you trust your staff, your school is on course in its wellbeing journey. Who is going to carry the wellbeing toolkit with you? Teachers? Support staff? Governors?

In Chapter 3 we will look in depth at the culture of the school, which, if you get it right, will build to make a genuine difference to wellbeing in the workplace.

Toolkit takeaways

This chapter has given us a broader approach to wellbeing, applying our values to our team building processes. Authentic values are there to be lived. Wellbeing lives through your values and your team can deliver those values.

- Celebration:
  - Give genuine thanks for going above and beyond.
  - Keep it real to keep it honest but make sure everyone is included.
- Collaboration:
  - Share and keep it fair.
  - Build your team to cope with times of adversity and challenge.
- Respect:
  - Have clear rules for respect.
  - Be visible.
  - Be a 'doer' not a 'teller' for the visible impact.
- Trust:
  - Drop the micromanagement; it is unworkable and breeds a tale-telling culture.
  - Let go and let people be interdependent.
- Support:
  - Challenge negative language and actions.
  - Actively and visibly promote positivity through coaching language.
  - Build your coaching network.
- Perseverance and resilience:
  - Model 'cool detachment' as a way of facing up to negative and challenging situations.
- Courage:
  - Act upon negative language.
  - Outlaw favouritism and have no favourites.
  - Never fear doing what you know to be right in promoting and protecting wellbeing.

- Empathy:
    - Conduct a carefully structured wellbeing survey.
    - Act on the survey results and be visible in the actions. Build resilience and model dealing with challenge.
- Time:
    - Simply protect it.

---

3 School culture: making wellbeing grow and thrive

Chapter overview

Through this chapter we will explore how positive relationships and an affirmative culture can be developed through a combination of action, attitudes and application of our toolkit values established in Chapter 2. This will be based in part on the model that we use at my own school.

We will then examine how 'toxic' environments can develop where wellbeing is not an area of priority with some specific scenarios, drawn from my research, which may surprise some readers. I go on to offer guidance as to how school leaders can avoid and overcome toxic school environments.

The final part of the chapter, also taken from survey responses, addresses the ultimate in 'toxicity': concerns in relation to bullying in the workplace. After outlining the forms that bullying can take, I offer additional specific guidance to challenging and eliminating such conduct.

Have you ever felt unwell during term time?
Have you called in sick or come in regardless?
Do you notice when a colleague is unwell?
What is your response?

If you interpret the first pair of questions as being targeted at teachers, teaching assistants and other staff and the latter pair as being directed at SLT, then read them again.

Still thinking the same thing? Or did you acknowledge that all four questions could be asked of the school workforce as a whole?

The perception we have of these questions reflects our experience of school cultures. As we will see in later chapters, decisions about policy and workload relating to planning, marking, feedback and assessment and the expectations attached to these will dominate many a staffroom discussion about teacher stress. It is how school leaders choose to manage these, or not, that will have a major impact on the pressures on our staff. However, if we are to take account of the 'sideways-in' model (see page 24), then surely we need to develop a culture in which every member of our staff looks out for each other and is aware of the impact that their words and actions have upon others.

Developing a positive culture

In an ideal world, as school leaders, we are hoping for all our staff to be in school every day of the 195 days expected of them in the public sector. As teachers, teaching assistants and school leaders we would be looking to attend every day too, because we know the difference we make to the lives of our children.

The world of education, as much as any workplace, however isn't ideal and staff absence is part of the ongoing management of a school. Even the hardened professionals who tell their young colleagues that they will catch everything from the children in the first five years before immunity to all known germs kicks in will occasionally succumb to an infection or virus. Physical illness or injury is relatively easy to identify for the sufferer. We can recognise when a colleague is struggling through a heavy cold or viral infection. In each case self-medication, rest or a visit to the GP will result in recovery.

Do we as leaders do enough to stop our teachers getting ill? There is little headteachers can do to prevent colds, flu or sickness bugs among their staff beyond the expected levels of workplace cleanliness. However, tiredness, lack of sleep and stress can make staff more vulnerable to illness. Part of the culture of positive wellbeing needs an 'eyes-open' approach to such circumstances. Do we work in schools where we will send unwell staff home, even though they may not have raised their illness with anyone or disguised it with paracetamol and a smile?

Whilst physical problems are easier to identify and treat, the more prominent issue is the mental wellbeing of our colleagues. We as educational professionals aren't trained to diagnose mental health issues, but we can perhaps identify situations where pressure, stress and deadlines can impact upon our colleagues. Resilience may be stronger in some colleagues than others. Whilst some may appear to be able to cope with any situation and weight of workload that comes their way, others may not have the regulatory skills to self-manage.

Some of our colleagues are more vulnerable than others. This is not something to be judgemental about; it requires compassion, understanding and humanity. To be empathetic with the vulnerability of others we need to understand vulnerability ourselves, to have lived and experienced it. Without a comprehension of vulnerability, you cannot manage and lead people.

Wellbeing, as we have already established, is for everyone and it is for every day. It needs to be applied equally and it needs to be nurtured and authentic. Wellbeing will develop where the culture of the school enables it to succeed. Some people are able to manage their own wellbeing; others cannot. Wellbeing shouldn't be delivered as a 'top-down' model because wellbeing actions will not suit everyone. Nor should it be 'bottom-up', as this has uncomfortable implications about school hierarchy, which, when it comes to mental welfare in particular, might challenge the equality of access to wellbeing.

The positive culture in which wellbeing can be supported isn't going to appear overnight. Those heads opening a new school have the chance to build from the ground up, but new heads in established schools with long-established staff may find changing the culture a challenge, especially where there has been negativity and cynicism before.

Being principled and consistent in upholding and communicating such values is a starting point. Such principles need to promote that good mental, physical and emotional wellbeing is essential and that everyone is appreciated and valued equally. Communication must be clear and transparent, concerns are discussed appropriately and taken seriously, and no individual, regardless of their role, should be judgemental of any colleague.

Ultimately the school culture needs to respect the most precious resource we have: time. Don't waste it through interminable meetings, needless initiatives and tasks with no useful outcome. Use the evidence of assessment, then reuse it, rather than demand retests that will only skew evidence. Trust your teachers to plan effectively and don't observe and monitor them more than really necessary.

Wellbeing and workload are not simple to manage and there will be challenges on the way. Evaluation, particularly of marking workload, needs to be in place and we need to be mindful of everyone in our team. Team spirit, standing by and standing up for colleagues, a positive culture and leaders who want to make this work provide the best foundations for a school where the wellbeing of the staff and children is truly valued.

Do you dare to create that positive culture?

We have dared to in my school. Let me explain how.

What is culture?

Schools depend on relationships between their stakeholders and, where these relationships are positive, schools will thrive. When a school hits the national press over an issue such as the lunch menu, banned haircuts, dance crazes or uniform, it may be the case of someone courting publicity for their complaint, but equally the relationship between school and community may have broken down. Trust is one of the most important bonding agents in any form of relationship. Parents need to trust the school to deliver the education they want for their child. The same level of trust needs to cascade through the institution.

Trust doesn't imply blind obedience. A level of challenge is healthy and is also a regular, if not daily, occurrence in school. How the challenge is presented will reflect upon the culture and level of trust. Where the challenge manifests itself in gossip and whispering in corners, the implication is that the trust isn't there and that positive relationships don't exist.

A school that is values driven can promote the positive culture that will promote wellbeing. The values will guide not only the curriculum but also behaviours of children and adults alike. 'Trust' is one of the core values in my school, so are 'hope', 'compassion', 'respect' and 'honesty' amongst others. The language and behaviours of each are expected of and embraced by everyone. Values permeate everything, from the way we address the children as they walk through the gate to the respect we show a colleague in times of stress, from celebrating successes of children and adults to protecting time for our teachers.

Wellbeing at my school is driven by six core principles that underpin our wellbeing policy and all decisions relating to the wellbeing of staff:

- a culture of positivity that all stakeholders contribute to equally
- an environment to energise all members of staff
- leaders who aim to be highly effective, proactive and non-judgemental
- excellent working relationships
- career satisfaction
- healthy lifestyle.

The model we have developed for staff wellbeing is one of 'sideways-in', where the whole community can take ownership of these six principles. This model will develop where the culture allows it to do so and this culture depends upon leadership mindset. We will explore each of the principles in turn, looking at the practical solutions that might work in different contexts to enable leaders to choose what may work in their setting.

A culture of positivity

At the core of the culture of positivity, there is a clear statement that respect and trust, shared purpose and clear channels of communication are at the heart of the school. As senior leaders we recognise that good mental, physical and emotional wellbeing is central to the best performance of our colleagues. Everyone is equally appreciated and valued because the engagement and commitment of everyone, teaching assistants, support staff, office staff as well as class teachers, are what we seek to achieve.

We actively encourage a positive atmosphere in the staffroom because we recognise that negativity is draining but positivity is catching. On our staffroom door the words 'Bring me sunshine in your smile' are prominent and though nobody as yet has attempted a Morecambe and Wise-style stage exit down the corridor, it cannot be ruled out. A positive quote appears on the staff newsletter each week and although there is some cynicism about motivational quotes on Twitter at times, we do place these in context, often relating them to events of the week just past.

Negativity, complaints and gossip should all be absent in a team culture and although this is a challenging aim we do encourage issues to be raised in an appropriate and non-critical forum. We have an open-door policy, but if someone has an issue, a grumble or concern, confidentiality is assured and everyone is certain that they will be listened to. We also aim to ensure that if one thing doesn't happen when and how it should, then it isn't a crisis because someone will always step up to the mark.

On page 47 we discussed how sometimes wellbeing needs some tough decisions. Here is one of ours: there is no culture of 'I…I…I' or 'me…me…me' and the loudest don't get their way. If we give in to the demands of the 'foot stampers', this would undermine the trust and respect that the rest of our colleagues have. 'I want' does not get a response; in fact it goes not to the bottom of the priority list, but to a different list entirely. A tough lesson, but it makes the point.

We back this with the use of positive language, however tired and tense we may be. Conversations do not begin with 'Can you…?' or 'I need…' but with 'Good morning' and 'How are you?', which are simple and effective in regard to wellbeing. Politeness costs nothing and sets people at ease; perceived rudeness can trigger anxiety and sets relationships on edge.

An energising environment

The environment in which we work contributes to how we feel. When it is supportive, it enables us to be relaxed, focussed and at ease. Where it is challenging, the alternative is irritation, cynicism, lethargy and disengagement. This includes everything from the classroom and office space we work in to formal and informal networks of support and efficient resourcing.

This is why we need a decent PPA space.

We place a strong emphasis on team spirit; 'there is no "I" in team', as an oft-quoted phrase goes, but to reiterate the avoidance of the first-person pronoun, we interpret every action as a contribution to the whole school community and not one of self-promotion. The weekly newsletter thanks individuals by name for what they have done above and beyond expectations and how it has benefited the school *per se*.

Meetings are kept to what is needed. A weekly business briefing, attended by teachers and support staff who are able to be there, on Friday at 8:30am clarifies the diary for the week ahead. Key deadlines are known up to a year in advance, assessment weeks and whole-school events in the main. We try to work to a 'nothing on less than two weeks' notice' strategy to allow plenty of time for cover to be set in place. Staff meetings are set at an hour, with prior notice if longer is needed (usually for a visiting provider), and are never held in the same week as parents' evenings or nativities. Acknowledging the time that our colleagues give elsewhere will demonstrate that they are being recognised and appreciated. If we take the approach that for everything additional we ask then we take something away, we can balance the wellbeing of our staff.

We also aim for clutter-free spaces, as clear spaces do enable a clear mind. Reflecting the expectations we have of our children we try to keep our limited spaces organised and tidy with a place for everything, where it can be found. Again little things like this promote the positive culture, where mess and disorganisation can make staff anxious and concerned.

Often the environment can be energised by the simplest of ideas. We have a team breakfast each Friday during our diary briefing. We take it in turns and the variety reflects the tastes of our colleagues; every crumpet is matched by a muffin or a tea cake, the occasional sausage sandwich balanced by the classic bacon butty. Friday lunchtime a couple of years ago began with 'Team Salad' where every participant brought a different ingredient. This transformed into 'Potato Friday' as the weather cooled: proper baked potatoes, done in the oven, with a variety of fillings again reflecting the tastes, cultures and backgrounds of the staff. Nobody is pressured to take part, but as with the breakfast it promotes a sense of togetherness and unity because the simple act of serving, sharing and eating together brings us together. We talk, we share and we find out things about each other.

The simplest and most effective thing we did for wellbeing is to purchase a four-pint teapot. Drawing upon the Healthy Toolkit 'Tea and Talk' initiative, making a pot of tea requires time to brew it, to pour it and to share out the mugs, which promotes time to talk. The talk isn't about children or parents, behaviour or Ofsted, but about each other, about trivialities, about the little things that make people tick – in other words about knowing each other.

Effectiveness of leadership

It is our stated intention to know our team well, professionally and personally. We don't need to know every specific detail of their lives, but there are some essential things to be aware of. Do you know who has children or grandchildren living abroad, who has parents who are aged or unwell, who has children at university or working towards important exams? Do you know who is a keen gardener, a talented cook, a bookworm or an amateur thespian? Are you aware if your colleague has a cat or dog that is unwell or close to the final visit to the vet? Knowing what goes on beyond the school day gives a clear picture of needs, wants, lives and loves. Our colleagues are humans with feeling, not soulless automatons programmed only to teach and churn out mere numbers.

Knowing your teachers, teaching assistants and support staff enables you to recognise when help and support are needed. This is because if you talk to your staff with face-to-face interaction you can recognise subtle changes in body language, facial expression and tone of voice. A simple 'Are you OK?' may result in a nodded affirmative or a burst of emotion, an emergency hug and a tear-soaked shoulder. Being there for your staff is important and appreciated. Knowing your staff also means you know their strengths and who you can delegate to without rocking the boat or causing any upset.

Good leaders are polite, polite enough to disguise an instruction as a suggestion. A simple choice of written or verbal language, in feedback for example, has a huge impact upon our teachers. Effective and appropriate feedback delivered in a discussion, rather than a monologue, is essential.

Strong leaders model healthy working habits. 'Nobody is going to give you a gold medal for working late,' as Dr Emma Kell memorably said at the first Teach Well Fest in the summer of 2018. Bookending the day is quite different from working late but to encourage leaving at sensible times gives a model that your teachers can follow.

Leaders should be non-judgemental of the words and actions of their staff. Some teachers will be grumpy, nonplussed or emotionless at an announcement. They are all different. For each person who flies off the handle immediately there will be the teacher who considers their reaction and may not give their honest reaction for days. For each colleague with conservative opinions there will be one who is more liberal in their thoughts. Our primary concern is who is doing an effective job, and if both examples do, what is the issue?

Genuinely caring for the wellbeing of those who work for us and with us is at the heart of the philosophy of leaders who truly value their staff. Appraisal and performance management as a supportive process designed to enhance career development, rather than something that is 'done to' staff, demonstrate this commitment unmistakably. Clear and unambiguous support for behaviour issues and the modelling of behaviour management strategies to less experienced staff further demonstrate a collaborative and supportive approach, especially when delivered in a non-critical and empathetic manner.

Class visits aren't just for observation and discipline. Visible leadership, 'management by wandering around' as Mary Myatt (2016) so eloquently describes it, actively demonstrates that the leaders' attention is on the bigger picture: the whole school and the wellbeing of everyone. How often do you as a school leader pop in to say hello to the staff and children? Or is every visit on your monitoring schedule? If every move is monitored, what is the degree of trust being shown?

The most approachable leaders are trusted and respected. Neither trust nor respect can be demanded and both need to be earned, by showing that trust and respect, and by showing that they can use their toolkit to actively promote a culture of wellbeing.

Excellent working relationships

Strong working relationships are central to wellbeing and resilience and can facilitate the building of trust and respect. The strongest relationships thrive on a healthy mix of support and challenge; they celebrate success, resolve conflict quickly and allow colleagues the responsibility to look out for one another during pressurising and demanding times.

We encourage our staff to come to the staffroom for lunch and breaks and we have a natural level of banter as part of a good team spirit. It is recognised that it doesn't suit everyone and nobody is judged for spending their lunchtime marking. Keeping an eye out for those who don't make a regular appearance is important; indeed it is part of knowing your staff.

We have also tried to have wellbeing buddies with varying degrees of success. After the first year where everyone was allocated a buddy, we allowed people to opt in the next year, as some people felt it wasn't quite working as they'd thought. The idea isn't to have a stream of gifts in the pigeonhole each week, but to ensure that everyone was being looked out for with kind words, a supportive comment here and there, anonymous notes of thanks and a word to leaders if there is a concern we may have missed. Ultimately the buddies are about reinforcing the culture of wellbeing belonging to everyone.

A simple initiative that proved a success at the end of a busy autumn term was our 'Secret Santa Wellbeing Advent Calendar'. Simple to organise and with workload only for Santa, it required only a shoebox covered in wrapping paper and a wrapped gift for everyone. Each working day through advent there was a gift in the box for one or two people, covering the whole staff through to the end of term. Nothing extravagant, but again a reflection on knowing your staff, the gift was something simple and personal to the recipient: a jar of olives, a box of green tea or a lottery scratch card. Simple, but effective.

Career satisfaction

It is important to us that there is career satisfaction for our staff; a teaching job is a calling as well as what pays the bills. Having the right stretch and challenge and training and support to develop skills and fair reward for the job are crucial. We don't want staff to feel overwhelmed by the demands and pressures of their role, as this would breed stress and erode resilience.

Teachers who are content with the pace they have to work at and feel confident in their ability to get the job done are more likely to be engaged and performing at their highest level. Professional development opportunities are available equitably across the school regardless of experience. Performance management isn't something 'done to' staff as a tick-box exercise. Rather appraisal cycles allow staff to consider their future career paths and how they can gain experience, qualifications and confidence. Everyone has the opportunity to gain and exercise some leadership opportunities, be they in a school-wide initiative, a special curriculum day or otherwise.

Healthy lifestyle

We seek to encourage a healthy lifestyle but we cannot dictate what 'healthy' looks like, only model it. A healthy lifestyle can determine our physical, emotional and mental wellbeing, both inside and outside work.

We don't want to hear of poor sleep patterns and bad eating habits that can arise during challenging times. Long hours, little time for any physical exercise, even less time for family and friends, and no time for supporting yourselves all risk burnout. So we encourage staff to have no more than two hours non-contact time in school, and senior leaders no more than three. 'Early Exit Fridays' were discussed but there were some colleagues who preferred to stay late on that day to complete their preparations for the coming week. Wellbeing really is about individual choice and respect for that choice.

We encourage email switch-off in the evenings and at weekends. There is only one email from me at the weekend, which has the weekly newsletter and diary of events for the week ahead. There is no requirement to respond to this email, as it is purely for information and never contains a request to do anything. The only proviso is that the email is read and understood before the start of school on Monday. If anyone sends an email at the weekend or in the evening, there is no obligation on anyone to answer it, though I do answer mine.

We also take time to model time management strategies and we have evaluated and implemented the workload initiatives, which are explored in Chapter 4.

*

That is what we do at our school. Call it idealistic if you wish but it works in our setting. It isn't perfect, but it is principled and constantly evaluated, and it aims to produce that positive working culture in which wellbeing can thrive. The values and principles are the hardest working tools in the toolkit.

Setting the positive culture

Try out the following steps in your school to develop a positive culture that will help wellbeing thrive. Remember, there is no one-size-fits-all approach here, so be sure to consult with your school staff and constantly evaluate what you are doing to build an effective strategy.

- Establish what is and what is not going to happen in your school and stick to it because inconsistency is your worst enemy.
- Establish a positive vibe in the language that you use and the image you portray.
- Build your school relationships:
    - Establish trust by showing trust.
    - Be genuine in your positivity – it isn't for show. Believe and act what you say.
    - Energise your team – bring them together as often as possible but not with enforced jollity.
    - Ditch the clutter.
    - Remember the value of a good cup of tea – Mrs Doyle was never wrong.
- As a wellbeing leader:
    - Be visible, really visible, in class, at the gate and in the hall, interacting with staff, children and parents.
    - Be genuine and authentic in your values and actions. Roll your sleeves up and get your hands dirty.

- Engage in meaningful conversation that goes beyond lesson observation and pupil progress.
- Watch out for who isn't around, who stays in class and who doesn't engage. Look out for their work–life balance.
- Model good working practices: have a regular clock-in and clock-off time and encourage some early departures.

- Use email carefully: at weekends for information only in one message. If something can be asked in conversation, talk about it, don't email it.

Case study: 'Look after your staff and they will look after you'

Parklands Primary School, Leeds

Chris Dyson has been the headteacher of Parklands Primary School since 2014. He took over a school with low expectations of its pupils and with similarly low staff morale. Exclusion numbers had been very high, and behaviour was poor, including the now infamous games of tag on the roof. Often described as the most deprived school in Britain, Parklands has 84 per cent of its children receiving free school meals. Chris inherited a staff used to a regular verbal battering behind closed doors. If the school had been inspected at that time, 'inadequate' would have been the most likely judgement.

Four years on and Parklands is Ofsted-rated 'Outstanding' and Chris is a regular at the TES Awards, collecting the prize for community collaboration in 2017. In that time, Chris has seen very little change in the make-up of his staff. How does he do it?

Chris loves a visitor at Parklands, adults and children. Arriving at his office at lunchtime, door wide open as it always is, with the exception of the most sensitive meetings, I was greeted by walls of notes, cards, pictures and gifts from the children. Children came and went, talked freely and honestly and enjoyed the friendly banter of their headteacher. Make no mistake though; they know Chris is in charge and they know their boundaries, but they also know that their wellbeing is at the top of the Parklands agenda.

Chris applies a similar attitude towards his staff. Little movement in the staff save for moves abroad and promotion is testament to the positive culture that Chris has grown. To keep hold of staff, young teachers in particular, at a time when some schools experience close to 100 per cent turnover each year or two, is an admirable achievement. He embraces the opportunity that part-time teachers offer. Whereas some heads would baulk at this prospect, at Parklands it is recognised that this is a means to retain staff, look after their wellbeing through reduced hours and reward them by trusting them. Though the Parklands Twitter feed is full of celebration, such as 'The Parklands Fun Palace' and the 'Best Seats in the House', and this would suggest that life is one long party, this is far from the case. Book looks and drop-in observations are conducted as rigorously as anywhere else. They are however accompanied and supported by an atmosphere in which teachers are coached and given constructive feedback, rather than in an environment of critique and fear.

'Look after your staff and they will look after you' is the Dyson philosophy, words echoed by the staff I spoke to. Days in lieu are granted for attending Saturday INSET and events such as Primary Rocks and Northern Rocks. Days off are also given to staff, teaching assistants included, who attend residential trips. In many schools this is not the usual practice at all. Time is given during the day for marking with a vital 20-minute window being opened for an assembly or PSHE lesson, enabling immediate feedback for the day's mathematics teaching. Teachers aren't expected to mark homework as it is either completed on an online platform or in the form of home projects. Written planning is not required, as planning and preparation time is given over to the production of flipcharts and teaching resources. Chris's young teachers feel like he wishes to empower them and that crucially he trusts them. One became an NQT mentor having just completed their first year of teaching, unheard of in some establishments, but here Chris provides an invaluable learning experience in giving the opportunity to lead from an early stage in one's teaching career.

There is a feeling of a very positive culture at Parklands. In Chapter 1 I discussed how wellbeing couldn't be covered in a training day. The Dyson way is to have a team-building day, a few days before the start of the autumn term in the last days of August. There is no compulsion to attend, again because of family commitments, holidays or simply because it isn't to everyone's taste, but the day of bowling, boating or laser tag is rewarded with time off in lieu also. Carried by the force of Chris's personality, most staff choose to attend this day. They feel a sense of team bonding, that Chris values them and that they begin the term on a positive note. Contrast this with the sometimes rather staid and awkward training day and team-building experiences described earlier in the book; the difference lies in choice for the members of the team and a very clear purpose for Chris.

It was intriguing to talk to the teaching assistants, many of whom had served through the two previous headteachers' appointments. Though they recognised Chris's role in forging the positive and vibrant culture that Parklands has at present, they all believed that they had a tight bond before he arrived. They felt this was important under the previous regime as during that time there was a lot of 'sneaking about' and tale telling to the head, staff crying in stock cupboards and a 'ruthless' attitude from the school leadership, where people feared for their jobs and their mental health.

The most refreshing aspect of the Dyson headship is his open-door policy and his very obvious desire to care and to put children first. Described as 'Brilliantly Bonkers', everyone feels able to challenge him if necessary but there is a degree of comfort and confidence in doing so. They might not always see entirely eye-to-eye, but nobody has their head bitten off. He has allowed teaching assistants the opportunity to work flexibly and childcare commitments are accommodated and written into working hours.

Chris Dyson is a character, as large and ebullient in real life as he is on Twitter, his assemblies are a performance, his energy engaging and his enthusiasm infectious; a spur-of-the-moment thinker with a passion for everything and anything that will benefit his school, his children and his staff. Ofsted agreed in their 2017 inspection report: 'The Headteacher is an inspirational leader who lives and breathes Parklands Primary School. His enthusiasm and ambition for pupils and the community are boundless'. The summary of the report recognises the trust and respect that exist and have grown between pupils, parents and staff.

Chris is also a man of great humanity and sensitivity, as one particular example demonstrates with great clarity. Many Twitter users will be familiar with Beth Bennett, and will know that she lost her husband in the summer of 2017, just as she was about to take on the role of SENDCo at Parklands. Beth called Chris when her husband was taken to hospital and again when he had passed away. Immediately Chris put in place a programme of support for Beth. He didn't require her to begin work in September but allowed her to set her own time when she felt ready.

Ofsted came in the second week of September and Beth came to meet the inspectors despite her recent loss. Chris has continued to support Beth to work flexibly in her semi-retirement. When I met Beth in 2018, her 'pinned tweet' summed up the support she has received in a sentence: 'I can never thank @chrisdysonHT enough for believing in me when I didn't and saving me from myself!'

Chris has the force of personality to drive his school forward; he shows a genuine care for his teachers and teaching assistants and uses an inspired and clearly values-led approach to the wellbeing of the whole school community. He is a wellbeing toolkit personified.

Challenges to culture and the roots of toxicity

Wellbeing cannot thrive in an atmosphere where unexpected pressures occur and unfairness is perceived. Ultimately it is the role of school leadership to challenge negativity, tackle unethical behaviours and develop the threads of a positive culture. There are many undesirable strands that have emerged in my research, both in online surveys and in face-to-face discussion, and I have quite deliberately filtered these inauspicious components into two categories: examples of behaviours and practices that contribute to a toxic school culture and the more specific examples of workplace bullying, which I will deal with on page 87.

Together, toxic behaviour, toxic practices and workplace bullying are contributing to the retention crisis, and I believe that this direct threat to the wellbeing of our teachers and support staff, as well as our senior leaders, is having a major impact on the ability of schools to keep staff not only in their institution but also within the profession. However, there are practical and values-centred solutions to toxicity that leaders can trial and embed in their schools, which I would like to explore further.

It's not fair!

Perceptions of unfairness influence our sense of wellbeing. The principal grumbles about fairness relate to time, such as loss of our valuable PPA time. Mainly postponed because of staff absence or professional development courses, there is little use however in receiving this precious time weeks or months later, as many teachers rely on it to free up their evenings or weekends.

Under the 'School teachers' pay and conditions' document (Department for Education, 2017a), we still operate to the 1,265 hours of directed time in theory; the figure of 1,265 hours has remained the same since I began teaching. In practice, we know that our teachers give many more hours than this. A Google search will show any number of directed time calculator tools, often as an Excel spreadsheet, for school leaders to use. One teacher told me that in a previous post the headteacher continually quoted this figure 'as though she needed to direct every hour. It gave the impression that if we weren't being directed we were obviously doing nothing.' Though unspoken, this says much for the culture at this school and by implication these teachers must have been made to feel uncomfortable. Using the directed hours calculation to determine teaching hours and open evenings is one thing; to employ it to say how many PTA events, school plays and prom nights your staff should attend begins to undermine trust. Get the culture right and the staff will support those events for the good of the children; get it wrong and you will find a few challenges.

Associated with time, workload is also a source of perceived unfairness. The three workload reports released in 2016 (see Chapter 1, page 14) make reasoned suggestions for reducing the burdens of marking, planning and data management. Implementing these will be discussed in some depth in Chapter 4, page 99. How many schools though have addressed these reports? In exploring the experience of other professionals, both in SLT and class based, I discovered that many schools hadn't acted upon the reports and that some weren't aware of their existence. These are useful and practical reports with which to start exploring issues of workload. To either not share these with our teachers or dismiss them with a sweeping 'this won't work' statement without due consideration will raise questions of fairness. Ofsted is refreshingly aware of the impact of workload, and of its role in adding to stress and anxiety. A tweet from Sean Harford at the end of August 2017 asked SLT how they would be addressing the issue in the coming year. Sean was most encouraged by the replies that he received. I'm not going to suggest 'Ofsted want to see it' but if Ofsted are interested in it, and contribute to the panels as Sean did, then surely it is fair to see what the reports suggest.

There are many schools that will use lots of wellbeing initiatives and ideas such as extra PPA time, working hours that can be spent at home, report writing days, a buddy system and a 'shout out' wall. These are all great ideas but if the school fails to address the real problem, which is the sheer amount of work expected and the pressure of 'being the best', this will create anxious staff who worry about the perception of their performance too much and therefore have less energy to exert in actual performance. A shift in culture will truly improve staff wellbeing.

The complexities of communication and the tyranny of email

Communication, where it isn't carefully considered, can impact upon wellbeing. Email, though efficient, can be impersonal and those who don't think before they send may appear rude or blunt. A round-robin email announcing a new initiative, a sudden and unexpected deadline or requiring additional work from teachers already burdened will cause resentment and likely generate pressure or unease. Where schools do not have an email 'curfew' it is not uncommon for staff to send and respond to emails late at night or weekends.

Unreasonable expectations eat into leisure times. Weekends and holidays should be protected from intrusions, yet the use of staff email in the evening encroaches on the off-duty times of our teachers. Emailing lesson plans, demands for policy updates, data analyses, reports on individual children: I have heard of all of these and they may well have been in your experience too. We are all entitled to a social and personal life, but we will all balance this with our professional duties. If there is an issue with planning, it surely needs to be addressed in school, face-to-face as part of professional development. Impersonal emails, encroaching into the time when we should be relaxing, add to a sense of apprehension, particularly if there are other issues with negative culture in the school.

My out-of-office email reply sets the tone for anybody emailing at unreasonable hours. Please feel free to copy verbatim.

Thank you for your email.

As part of our whole-school commitment to wellbeing there is no expectation for our staff to read or answer emails sent between 6pm and 7am in the week, or at any time at weekends or during the holidays.

Should your email not receive an immediate reply, this is not a case of being impolite but one of choosing wellbeing ahead of workload.

Thank you.

Taking your staff email account off your mobile phone is liberating. In fact this is something all heads should tell their staff to do. The 'ping' of notifications on a smartphone can be irritating, especially in company, but the 'buzz' announcing an email, particularly with an ill-thought-through subject heading brings the worry of the workplace to time at home with loved ones or to an evening out. Signing in from a laptop at least gives your teachers the option of deciding when to read their email.

The read receipt is another aspect of emailing to consider in your wellbeing toolkit. We would all like to know when something has been read and I am sure you have all had the 'I didn't see that email' conversation, but placing a read receipt request again has implications about trust, or the lack of it.

Communication is always a thorny issue in school, especially if a message doesn't get through. Email may be efficient, but lacks the personal touch if we type in the same manner and style that we employ when texting or using WhatsApp. The value of a face-to-face conversation, clarity of explanation and taking the time to make a point is that these things show a human touch. Does everything have to go in an email?

How do your members of staff talk to each other?

Place anywhere between ten and 100 people in a room and ask them to get on with each other instantly and for the next few weeks and months. Your chances of this being a success are pretty low. Add high-pressure tasks, arbitrary deadlines, external judgements and the fear of failure, and the chance of two people not exchanging some harsh words becomes more unlikely.

This isn't however the 'Big Brother' house or some other contrived reality show. This reality is happening in many of our schools as many of our teachers and leaders forget how to address each other.

Many teachers told me that they have been shouted at; not 'talked to' but 'shouted at'. Typically this might be behind the closed doors of the head's office, but many have reported that this has been in public view, in the staffroom or along the corridor. It is not just in the realm of the headteacher either. Teachers have reported being 'yelled at by the maths leader because I hadn't updated my Progress 8 predictions on the spreadsheet' and were equally perturbed that colleagues in the staffroom had heard this reprimand too. Another primary-based teacher in Year 6 was rebuked at the staffroom table by the English lead for 'missing the target' on an end-of-term SATs practice test. Both these examples are clear indications of wellbeing being undermined by the words of others, doubly so because of the public nature of the rebuke. It is also a gauge of the pressure that high-stakes testing puts on all of us. Let us be slightly generous to the shouters for a moment; the pressure is on them too. What is clearly lacking here is any element of empathy for the feelings of their colleagues.

You may have witnessed teachers or teaching assistants who have to work together but have fallen out over an issue that may have been insignificant but in the pressure-cooker environment of the test season magnifies to something catastrophic. It is like, as one respondent said, 'watching two people going through a divorce but still having to live in the same house'. Secondary colleagues tell me that this is a frequent occurrence within departments and in primary where the head sees data but doesn't have an appreciation of the learning needs of the class or of the curriculum. That wave of pressure hits the staff who have fallen out but it is then for their colleagues to face the consequences of this. The wellbeing of several parties is under threat here, including those who have only been indirectly involved to this point. The positive culture of wellbeing is further under threat here from examination pressure but also the lack of interpersonal skills by one or more in this chain.

Relationships between staff

In Chapter 2, page 33, while discussing values, I raised the importance of relationships in school, meaning the professional and interpersonal relationships that are at the core of our wellbeing toolkit. Intimate and romantic relationships (there is a difference) between staff are another matter, one that can have a significant and possibly damaging impact upon the wellbeing culture of a school and that can undermine trust and respect.

Let's be very clear. It is so very important that all our teachers and other staff have a right to a private life and to a romantic life. It completes them; it is one of life's inevitable consequences. When we hear of students in ITT being told that they won't have time for a personal life, this is nonsense. Having a significant other, particularly in our profession, is ever so important. It grounds you, gives you a sense of reality and tells your children and parents that you are a caring person, especially when you become a parent.

Relationships begin in many a workplace. We will all know a couple who met at work. We should not be surprised if our young teachers pair up at college or in their initial appointment at school. It is a natural human response; young people pair up. We all love a wedding, civil partnership, christening or welcoming ritual! My A-level history teachers were a married couple, Pauline and Chris Collier, a wonderful and inspirational pairing who inspired my lifelong love of the subject.

There comes a point though when a relationship between two members of staff may be good for their wellbeing, but not for that of their colleagues. That point comes when there is a suggestion of favouritism or of social exclusion. One teacher said that as one of three newly qualified teachers, a naturally supportive bond developed both within school and socially. However, after the other two paired up, the social exclusion began, the support dropped and when the couple gained additional responsibilities at the expense of the third, a sense of resentment set in.

Favouritism, or a perception of it, does trigger anxiety. So too does the notion that two teachers in a relationship may be discussing school matters as 'pillow talk' particularly where one partner is in a position of seniority. One teacher in my survey complained that in their school the senior partner would 'listen to every complaint the younger one had' and take that issue and a series of petty points and lambast their colleagues at length 'usually late on Friday or once at the end of term', the timing of which is only going to start the weekend or holiday in the worst way possible.

The biggest fear that teachers have of close personal relationships is the element of 'power', especially if one or both are in senior leadership. Some schools do have a policy in regard to relationships, which may either suggest being discrete or that one partner moves on, which would be sensible to avoid any issue or grievance. Romantic relationships are not an area that we can legislate for, but one we need to be aware of at both the 'making up' and 'breaking up' stages and how this can feed gossip and a cliquey culture.

Cliques and gossip

Cliques in the workplace can challenge authority and where they exclude others, socially or professionally, they challenge wellbeing too. A group who socialise together aren't necessarily a clique in a large secondary school, for example; each department may be close knit and interactions between them limited. If a group dominates in the staffroom, however, by volume or physical presence, this can intimidate and sideline other colleagues. What causes concern to our colleagues is when that group then appears to have some power and influence.

A primary teacher said that in their school, the Year 6 team had the ear of the head, more so than might be expected for the SATs year. The group became very closed and secretive, the data manager wasn't able to access their information and there was an unfair allocation of resources, physical and human. When staff complained to the head, they found themselves marginalised socially and professionally, shouted down in staff meetings and their previously well-regarded teaching belittled.

Gossip and breaches of personal or professional confidentiality can arise through the existence of cliques. Many teachers reported that their career, their relationships and other aspects of their private business became a source of interest and discussion. While there are many who will discuss all their business openly, there are plenty who guard their privacy. A culture of whispering in corners undermines the trust that individuals have in their colleagues.

In my survey results, there were some particular examples of toxic conversations, which cliques were often at the heart of. One example fell into the 'who is working the hardest' category, with a number of teachers reporting that the hours they kept were judged and discussed by those who stayed much later. If someone leaves at four o'clock, are they working any less hard than someone who leaves at six o'clock? Conversely there were other teachers who found themselves on the wrong end of discussions for being in the minority for working longer hours, creating great displays and taking pride in their work. These teachers' wellbeing was being impacted by unfair comments, such as implications that they were seeking the favour of the headteacher. There is no competition in school to see who is working the hardest. My response to this kind of comment is: 'There are people who work hard and there are people who tell you how hard they work.'

Several teachers told me that they found they were being criticised for taking their holidays in holiday time. It is for nobody else to comment on this. How you use your time is your choice. As Patrick Ottley-O'Connor, a great wellbeing advocate, told me, 'I tell my staff to plan their holidays as meticulously as they plan their working week.'

As leaders, we need to be aware of such cliques and find ways to dissolve them, because anything that causes discomfort and worry has an adverse impact upon wellbeing.

The staff night out: not everyone's cup of tea?

The staff night out and other social events might not, at first sight, appear to be a concern regarding wellbeing in schools. After all, the notion of staff socialising together, not 'talking shop' but engaging in conversations and social interactions they might not otherwise be involved in at school, would certainly go some way to addressing the principles of collaboration and celebration. To bring the team together to mark the successful end of a term or a school year in a different environment on the surface would seem a positive step towards wellbeing. School leaders should, however, be aware that this seemingly innocent event can be tinged with the toxic side of office politics and be a source of anxiety for some members of staff.

One question I asked in gathering material for this book regarded cliques and social exclusion, in which I anticipated answers referring to domination of the staffroom and whispering in corners. Whilst those aspects are addressed on page 77, many of the responses I received specifically mentioned social events as an area where staff felt excluded and that in many cases their social standing in school was undermined by behaviours they had witnessed or experienced. Though offsite events are a grey area in terms of staff discipline and behaviour, the impact of exclusion from social occasions and the experience some staff have need to be considered by leaders within the broadest definition of wellbeing.

Social exclusion is unpleasant for anyone who has experienced it. As teachers, we act to support children who are left out and to deal with the miscreants as part of how we address any bullying issues in school. When social exclusion starts creeping into working life shouldn't we consider similar strategies for addressing it?

One theme raised was how inclusive school social events are. One teacher, from a school with a large staff of 60, reported that an end-of-year social was organised with just 20 places. Immediately this spells out that there is an 'in-crowd', which by implication suggests an 'us and them' mentality, and that can only be divisive. Another response mentioned that the SLT organised events at places of their choosing, which priced out main-scale teachers and support staff who were unable to afford an expensive venue. These occasions were also organised for mid-week, a problem for those with young families but also at a time when staff were completing assessments and gathering data. Any sense of collaboration swiftly vanishes in this scenario.

Support staff, teaching assistants in particular, often reported feeling excluded in social situations, especially where they felt senior leaders did not value the contributions they made to the running of the school. On the other hand, teachers and SLT reported that they felt that support staff were organising their own events almost as a challenge to a notion of collaborative working. This occurred particularly where a new headteacher was trying to make their mark, but long-established staff were testing the waters, as is mentioned on page 48. The result was that some schools had two nights out on the same or consecutive nights and any sense of community and celebration was muted.

It is also apparent that some individuals have been isolated from social events, it being made clear that their attendance was unwelcome. Reasons given were gender (both female and male staff reported this), age, position (more than one headteacher hadn't been invited to their own Christmas bash) and, in one charmless example, 'because you're boring'. Whilst grown adults conducting themselves in this way seems beyond belief, the failure to act upon complaints is unacceptable too.

A further aspect of social exclusion is the gender-specific social occasion: the 'girls' or boys' night out'. Male-only events were mentioned only by secondary school teachers and were often department specific. Whilst not wishing to stereotype some groups of teachers, PE departments were referred to as promoting 'lad culture' on nights out, the more unsavoury side being when derogatory and sexually belittling comments about female staff are made. Not only should such remarks obviously not be made, being heard means that they might be, and usually are, reported back. Rumour, gossip and conjecture are also discordant and hurtful.

The behaviour of SLT on social occasions has also been called into question. Aside from the above example, examples cited have included the headteacher and other senior leaders gathering at one end of the communal table or seated away from the rest of the group, either engaged in their own conversation and not engaging in conversation or interacting with others. A number of teachers felt they were being watched or judged and several reported that their behaviour was commented upon by senior staff back at school. Staff social occasions are celebrations of the working environment, but they are not held in the working environment or indeed in working time. Should events during social occasions be used in disciplinary procedures? It depends on the offence given and taken; the demon drink is often a factor to consider.

The most disruptive factor on a staff night out, particularly at the end of a long, tiring and stressful year and where there have been undercurrents of discontent, is alcohol. There is no suggestion here that we ban drink from staff social events, but the fact is that tongues loosen and so do inhibitions. Whilst many of us can take a gentle ribbing, the most uncomfortable experiences reported to me in my survey included:

- Drinks poured over the heads of teachers, some of whom were SLT, and in one case a teacher was slapped around the face with a hot towel from a Chinese restaurant.
- A very loud declaration that two staff members were 'seeing' each other; they certainly were not and the word used wasn't 'seeing' either.
- A young and shy member of staff doing his best to avoid the unwanted and increasingly loud teasing from a teaching assistant eventually asking to be left alone only to be told, 'Why don't you just f*** off then', at which point he left the venue. He was later asked to foot his share of the bill.

The relationship to wellbeing is that in each case the people on the receiving end of the treatment by others had to face their colleagues the next morning. In each of these cases no action was taken by the headteacher. Was this because it was out of hours and beyond the remit of disciplinary procedures? Each victim reported feeling uncomfortable on entering the staffroom, none received an apology and all of them left their schools within a few months. The person victimising the young male member of staff eventually left, but only after repeated instances of embarrassing conduct both in and out of school.

Other occurrences on social occasions that caused upset, discomfort and anxiety included:

- The posting of pictures on social media, Facebook in particular, which could be viewed by parents or children, without permission and often left open to misinterpretation.
- Unwelcome, often sexist, comments, about dress sense, shoes and make-up; male staff and senior leaders were most often mentioned.
- Conduct requiring intervention of the management of the premises due to complaints from other customers.
- Inviting former members of staff who had been involved in personality clashes and disputes during their time at the school.

Whilst this remains an area over which disciplinary procedures and staff conduct may be ambiguous, there is no doubt that concerns over social occasions do impact wellbeing in the broadest context and as school leaders we need to be aware of the anxieties arising from them and the bearing they may have on relationships within the school.

The use and misuse of social media

As a means to develop a professional learning network and to build connections, Twitter is an amazing tool for teachers. With reduced budgets for professional development, EduTwitter has become an ideal platform to network, to learn and to share. It has fuelled a growth in teacher blogging and scheduled 'chats' on aspects of subject and school leadership. Furthermore it has encouraged the planning of teacher-led professional development, through local TeachMeets and regional or national Saturday conferences. Organisations such as WomenEd and BAMEed Network have built from a social media basis and of course we founded Healthy Toolkit through the same medium.

Both Facebook and Twitter provide supportive environments to ask for and offer professional help and opinion. Professional forum groups on Facebook and elsewhere allow teachers to expand their professional expertise through online interactions. One respondent indicated that it had allowed them to 'cultivate my own tribe' and to 'interact with others who contribute to my emotional and mental wellbeing' where this was absent from the work setting.

There are some healthy and lively discussions on Twitter. There are also some very unpleasant conversations online between education professionals, which will not be discussed here other than to mention that this has triggered anxiety issues for some tweeters who felt their opinions were being unfairly challenged. However, there are two categories of tweets that do relate to the principles of *The Wellbeing Toolkit*: threats to expose someone's anonymity or to report the tweeter or blogger to their school.

In the May half term of 2018, there was a suggestion on Twitter that an anonymous blogger had been suspended because of the content of their blog. Whilst no names were mentioned, there was discussion that the posts had been critical of the blogger's school and its leadership. Of course this entire thread could equally have been genuine as much as 'fake news', but this need not concern us here. What we should consider is how social media is 'monitored' in some schools and how this concerns the wellbeing of our staff.

By 'monitoring' I mean looking at someone's social media posts whilst not being a 'friend' or 'follower'. Whilst it is accepted that some employers, including schools, will look at social media usage to gauge the professional positive impact that a potential employee may have, what is not acceptable is looking at their profile once in role, whichever platform that person participates in. If a group of teachers want to be 'friends' on social media that is a personal choice; some people prefer not to 'follow' their colleagues, choosing instead to remain private. Privacy however does not mean having to 'lock' profiles.

My survey indicated several teachers who knew that other colleagues had looked at their Twitter or Facebook accounts. To blame is the smartphone with its scrolling and touchscreen technology. The evidence came in the form of notifications of 'follows' and 'likes' and then finding these being undone. Often these occurred late at night, particularly at weekends, the notifications only being spotted the following morning. There is a phenomenon in some circles called the 'drunken follow', which in essence means that somebody, or maybe a couple or group, have a look at the social media of a colleague whilst emboldened by a glass too many of a favoured tipple. It is all too easy for a touch on the screen to trigger a notification and even undoing an action doesn't prevent the alert being sent.

Other teachers commented on how seemingly innocent conversation in the staffroom clearly indicated that their posts had been spied upon, with comments such as, 'Did you enjoy your meal at...' or 'I never realised you liked...,' evidencing that their posts had been registered by people who maybe should not have been looking. Any person who posts from an account that isn't private is of course potentially letting anyone with online access read what they have to post. However other teachers and school staff aren't just anyone; they are trusted professionals in positions of responsibility. This isn't mild curiosity; this is stalking.

This can impact upon mental health by triggering anxiety and feelings of paranoia that a teacher and aspects of their life are being discussed and that this is also happening outside the workplace and usual working hours, especially if the teacher is a private person who doesn't discuss the small details of their life in the staffroom. Where the comments are made in a snide or sarcastic manner, confidence can be deeply undermined. The most potent example of this was of a teacher who posted pictures of a Saturday night out only to be called in by a member of SLT for doing so when their colleagues were 'up until midnight writing reports'. Whether they were or not is not of relevance to this particular teacher who had been up at six o'clock in the morning writing reports so that they could enjoy a social life.

In this case the 'spying' was by another teacher and the victim felt that this was an attempt to push them from the school, which was the eventual result. This has been a recurring theme where one member of staff tells tales to senior leaders about social media posts and pictures in order to discredit a colleague. This has been perpetrated by teachers, support staff and sometimes by senior leaders and in a number of cases heads had directed a member of staff to 'keep an eye' on the online activity of colleagues.

The nature of social media leads to sometimes wild and inaccurate speculation by those reading tweets, particularly when they are read out of context or out of sequence in an exchange. Regular tweeters will know that a locked or blocked account's tweets will not appear in a thread. Any snoopers will therefore have little idea of context. However, one response indicated being rebuked and threatened with action for 'liking' a post on Facebook and another teacher was called in for posting the words 'not happy' and being accused of letting down the school. The context of this related to a domestic concern, which again was private, and there was no wish to discuss it at school.

If some members of staff are spending their leisure time scrolling the Twitter and Facebook timelines of their colleagues and dissecting who they interact with, there are questions to ask about their motivation. Sometimes the prying eyes of siblings or partners were at work. The feeling was that they were trying to get their colleagues into trouble or worse. If there was a genuine concern, for example a safeguarding issue, or something that brought the school into disrepute, such as being critical of a policy or an individual, then further action is quite justified. If this amounts to trouble stirring though, the actions of the stalker need bringing to account.

We can't expect our teachers to lead their lives without social media. If you have staff in their twenties, they may have lived a life sharing everything on a social network. More mature colleagues may be more circumspect but this can't be guaranteed either. Realistically, directing staff in their use of social media cannot be demanded, although I have heard of staff codes of conduct with highly restrictive rules and expectations, enough to make it near impossible to use.

Teachers are entitled to a life and equally entitled to lead that life on Facebook or Instagram if they wish to. Providing they don't embarrass the school or breach teachers' standards, there shouldn't be an issue. We discussed above the stalking of teachers on social media by their colleagues. Being viewed by parents is regrettably going to occur and the use of social media by parents or pupils to stalk, harass and threaten teachers is another matter entirely, particularly in regard to wellbeing.

In August 2018 a teacher was banned indefinitely because of Facebook posts including foul and abusive language (*TES*, 2018). What caught the teacher out was that the post was reported to the school by a parent; even though it didn't use the teacher's name, it was identifiable as them. We don't know how the parent found the post, but by the standards of this case their actions were commendable.

What if there are parents with other motivations, however? What is there to stop a parent finding a teacher on social media and contacting them with the potential to be at best intrusive and at worst abusive? We can't answer these questions, but we can anticipate how we might protect our colleagues if this occurs.

The danger with social media is the way it can allow many to pile in with their thoughts and opinions on an issue to which the context isn't understood, or is twisted to a venomous agenda. Sadly, social media can lead to public naming and shaming. With schools it often begins with uniform, haircuts or school dinners; 'school has rules, school applies rules' in short.

Where the words become directed not at schools but at individual teachers, this becomes more serious. If the individual accounts have been stalked by parents, then the potential is there for teachers to receive such posts directly. The potential for such actions needs schools to be proactive in anticipating this. A clear and unambiguous message needs to be conveyed: that if there is a genuine complaint in regard to an issue in school, there are procedures to follow that do not involve taking to social media to name the school or individual teachers. Although as an inclusive institution we don't want to bar parents from site, this needs to be clear as a possible consequence.

The primary reason for such a statement shouldn't be protecting the name of the school but safeguarding the wellbeing of our colleagues. Imagine the stress to receive abusive notifications on their phone or to be made aware of screenshots of such posts. If aware that this has gone on, keeping it secret from the staff wouldn't be advised because inevitably they will find out that it has happened. Transparency is important. The best means of protecting our staff is telling them not to look for the posts because to find them and read them would be upsetting. The protection of our staff's feelings is at the core of good wellbeing and the promise and sight of action will reaffirm the willingness of the school leadership to protect their staff.

Schools should also make it clear that they will not accept or listen to reports made from teachers outside of the school about the actions or opinions of staff on social media. There have been, sadly and a little shamefully, people with an education background making reports anonymously to schools about tweets, blogs and Facebook posts, as well as some making direct approaches to schools and headteachers through tweets. Reasonable and reasoned heads won't give time to such shabby tactics.

Sensible guidelines on the use of social media and what to believe from what is posted there makes for a good wellbeing INSET session. As a source of myth, rumour and fake news, social media is a potential challenge to wellbeing. If used well and if directed to the most objective material, wellbeing can be positively supported by it.

Other aspects of social media usage that impacted upon wellbeing for the respondents of my research survey included:

- One member of staff posting a derogatory comment about another on Twitter. SLT taking them aside to find out why they were unhappy, not disciplining them and their victim not even getting an apology.
- A teacher and their partner discussing another teacher on Facebook and no action taken by the headteacher.
- Teachers 'friending' parents on Facebook and confidentialities breached as a result.
- Feelings of stress and anxiety because of a school Facebook page with unrestricted settings, allowing parents to post challenging comments about staff.
- WhatsApp and Facebook groups used to discuss colleagues out of school hours, sometimes in derogatory terms. This is particularly so with SLT groups but also with groups of support staff.

- Such groups also being used to reinforce social exclusion, leaving one or more staff off the group. These teachers were made aware of what was going on by members of the group who at least had the decency to tell them.
- Teachers posting on Facebook that they had gone out socially 'because they had been working so hard' but deliberately not inviting another teacher, making them feel inadequate and anxious.
- In one of the most troubling cases, a staff member being discussed by name in a closed group by ex-colleagues and former and current parents of a school. Though this was removed, the reputational damage remained. Other teachers have reported unjustified and unqualified personal attacks without support from their school leadership.

Such intrusions indicate a particularly toxic culture in a school because they signify a lack of trust in teachers. We all have social media usage policies in our schools and in most cases the wording is in essence: 'Don't post anything that identifies children or embarrasses the school.' Which person has the time to look through the timelines of their colleagues and to produce printed screenshots? What is the setting of their moral compass to cherry pick posts from the past and what, safeguarding aside, would be the purpose of this? Would you as a school leader advocate the use in a disciplinary meeting of something that is essentially an act of stalking?

Challenging negative culture

A negative school culture can take many different forms and has a number of different triggers, from a perceived lack of fairness through to a misuse of social media. To avoid a negative culture festering in your school, try working on the following:

- Be visibly and candidly fair:
  - With PPA time: it is statutory, so don't let it be lost or wasted.
  - With the 1,265 hours: quoting this is a red rag; teachers fulfil this easily, so raising this banner implies a lack of trust.
  - If you're lucky, or financially prudent, with any extras in time, resources and free gifts.
- Set your email policy and stick to it. Don't send emails at weekends and out of school time, unless it is purely to give information.

- Set the same rule for WhatsApp groups.
- Be very clear about how your staff talk to each other. Set the visible example and challenge every incident. Challenge gossip. Challenge unwarranted criticism of teaching or lifestyle.
- Be aware of cliques and any favouritism or exclusion and challenge it.
- Set your stall on staff nights out very clearly: there should be no exclusion but also no expectation for all to attend.
- Set very clear rules about the use and misuse of social media.

Bullying in the school workplace

Bullying goes on in most workplaces in some form or other. Sadly it occurs in schools too as a hefty proportion of my respondents attest to. Bullying is an insidious element within the most toxic school cultures and may equally result from that culture as much as feed that toxicity.

Clearly defining bullying is challenging because one person's interpretation of their own actions will differ considerably from that of the recipient of the words and deeds. Just make the comparison for a moment of dealing with a bullying incident with a child. Even the very youngest are able to throw up defence mechanisms, deflection tactics and denials, or, in the case of the victim's allegations, exaggeration and a liberal interpretation of the facts may ensue. To a more sophisticated adult brain, such learned behaviours can often be ingrained and tough to crack. As we will see in this section of the book, this particular element of human nature can, without the values that the toolkit employs, bring toxicity to a head.

Let us try to define bullying of staff in school in simple terms. If someone is placed in unreasonable fear of the security of their job, that is bullying. If a person is undermined on a regular basis, criticised unjustifiably, embarrassed publicly by a colleague in relation to the performance of their role or simply embarrassed in public by some degree of personal criticism, then these too are representative of bullying. Being socially excluded, unfairly treated in monitoring cycles or in career advancement or discriminated against in terms of gender, sexuality, race, marital status or parental status all fit the same definition.

Challenging performance is not harassment, nor is the use of support plans an example of victimising a teacher. Setting targets, setting deadlines and changing policies are likewise not bullying. However, the manner in which these are done can be identified as bullying if there is the merest hint of the unfair application of expectations or if somebody is being hounded.

Though the intention of *The Wellbeing Toolkit* was not to create a piece of action research, a study into bullying in education was drawn to my attention. Declan Fahie and Dympna Devine (2014) of University College Dublin conducted 24 interviews about bullying behaviours in primary schools in the Republic of Ireland with reference to the impact upon the victims of bullying, both class teachers and headteachers. I read this study after my surveys had closed and I was startled to find that the manifestations of bullying behaviours almost entirely matched my own findings.

In the study, examples of derogation and exclusion listed were:

- abusive and intimidating behaviour
- rumour mongering
- sexual harassment
- shouting and yelling
- insulting and demeaning behaviour
- ignoring
- physical assault.

Pressurised and oppressive management regimes were typified by:

- trivial criticisms of work
- changing deadlines
- threatened job loss
- cyberbullying
- unreasonable job demands
- taking the credit for another's work
- threats to professional reputation.

All bar the physical assaults were reported in my survey responses. All represent a threat to the wellbeing of our staff and it is the responsibility of those with their wellbeing toolkit to hand to act upon these intimidatory behaviours and actions and to embed positive behaviours into the school culture.

Headteachers and SLT

Many responses to my surveys indicated that bullying and similar behaviours were carried out by headteachers and senior leaders. However, 'SLT bashing' will be familiar to many who have seen some discussions on certain sections of Twitter, Facebook and the forum pages of the *TES*. Heads who replied to my questioning also reported that such complaints had been directed towards them on several occasions. They felt that it was very easy for the word 'bullying' to be thrown into conversation and that they faced accusations of it particularly in dealing with competency or professional misconduct cases when in fact these circumstances were quite justified.

Asking somebody to complete a particular task isn't bullying, certainly not a task that is part of a teacher's responsibilities. Directing them to do this within a short time period in itself isn't bullying either, though it could be an example of poor management. When the task set is unfair, for example one teacher alone is asked to complete it whilst others are not, it is then beginning to move towards more dubious grounds. Repetition of this kind of behaviour towards the same teacher or group of staff members would definitely fit the description of bullying as defined on page 87.

There were many teachers who replied to my bullying survey saying that they had experience of a headteacher being involved in a clique, as part of a regime that was characterised by micromanagement and that was fuelled by rumour and gossip. Others advised that there were 'untouchable' members of the senior team who were immune from criticism, even after complaints about their professional conduct. When such cliques have a position of power, the culture in the school becomes one that is corrosive and critical and where self-interest and self-preservation come to the fore.

Wellbeing cannot possibly thrive in such circumstances. Teachers vote with their feet in schools like this, at least looking out for their own wellbeing but still leaving a system with toxicity at the heart of it.

Middle leaders

Middle leaders came out of the survey results quite poorly. Is this because middle leadership is an ill-defined role? A head of department in an urban comprehensive, particularly of maths or English, does not have the same responsibilities as a science leader in a primary school in the same authority, yet both may find themselves described as middle leaders and on the same training course. Is there greater focus on the word 'middle' or on 'leader'? What we may be finding is that one or neither is clearly defined.

Does the word 'leader' in a job title give licence to change your approach to your colleagues? Holding someone to account doesn't involve shouting at them, embarrassing them and undermining them in front of other teachers or sometimes before children. Does 'empathy' appear anywhere on their leadership training or indeed in their initial teacher training?

One teacher reported being bullied as an NQT by a middle leader who would make derogatory comments about resources and teaching materials, roll their eyes and tut within the sight and hearing of others and talk over the young teacher in staff meetings. Another was told by one middle leader that they were not a team player and that the rest of the department followed suit in their manner and conduct. Others reported an unfair number of observations, book scrutinies where books would disappear for a week and then be delivered without feedback, and capability proceedings being used as a threat to push someone out. Observation feedback with relatively insignificant items highlighted at the cost of useful comments about the quality of the teaching and learning was also a feature of some of the negative behaviours seen from middle leaders.

Why do middle leaders come out so poorly in my responses? There are three reasons. The first is the culture in which they work. If they have senior leaders who are negative and critical and who undermine colleagues, then this will be the model that they have to work upon. If the language and culture of the school are such, and if empathy is lacking, they will follow the example they have worked with. The second relates to ambition and many teachers have responded saying they felt that their middle and senior leaders acted this way to 'get in with the head' and to advance their own careers. Sad to think that emulating the actions of a bullying headteacher will help with career advancement. Sadder though is that the etching of these habits into these leaders' psyches does not bode well for the culture of wellbeing. The third reason comes in part from observation within my personal experience. At a previous school a combination of 'significant' birthdays, career breaks for raising a family, moving on to other schools or simply getting out of the profession left the school with a staff profile that consisted of teachers under the age of 28 or over 40, with nobody in the middle ground. Discussion with colleagues elsewhere, in both primary and secondary sectors, has suggested that this is a pattern repeated more widely. The implications are that we are missing that territory and range of experience where we might expect our middle leaders to come from. Chatter on teacher social media suggests that some teachers are taking on middle leadership roles in their second year of teaching. That is not to doubt their capabilities of growing as a leader but they will require that level of empathy that will nurture their compassionate side too.

Teacher on teacher

On page 77, I discussed the existence of cliques. Some of my teacher respondents reported experiencing and witnessing bullying by cliques. Often this takes very petty forms – hiding crucial items such as a USB stick or a resource needed for an observed lesson, taking lunches from the fridge or rearranging the classroom furniture – but it has a gradual impact upon their wellbeing over time. There is a thin line between having a joke and upsetting somebody's impeccable preparation. When the line is clearly crossed by those who use sexualised language and sexist behaviour, as was also reported, the reaction becomes not one of discomfort but one of sexual harassment.

Others reported negative behaviours beginning after an appointment to a role and a level of professional jealousy. One teacher, on promotion to a phase leader role, found that a person who was disgruntled despite not applying for the post suddenly became very critical of performance in lesson observations, where there had been no issue before and where the judgement by others remained as high as before.

Other teachers have reported incidents such as the spreading of false rumours, blame being falsely attributed and names being crossed off lists for social events. Again these are very petty, but when one particular young teacher reported such things to a line manager the concerns were dismissed and the recipient told to 'toughen up' and show some resilience. Empathy is here lacking again, from the bullies and the senior leader, and the resilience and wellbeing of the young teacher not being supported.

Another young teacher hadn't realised, out of naivety, for several months that the treatment she received was an example of bullying. Constant criticism, snide comments about age, dress, hair and make-up, being talked over and belittled in meetings all came from a teacher who had previous form like this but who had never been formally dealt with. Even after a complaint was raised, the conduct continued albeit to other victims. Headteachers need to take allegations of bullying behaviour seriously and visibly demonstrate what is not acceptable in their wellbeing culture.

Support staff

One aspect of the question about experience of bullying that surprised me was the level of complaint made both by heads and SLT, as well as classroom teachers, about the conduct of support staff.

The principal complaint from headteachers was of their support staff being the most prominent and vocal 'blockers' of changes they wished to introduce. In a scenario that will be familiar to many school leaders who have tried to implement a significant change of policy or direction, it will come as little surprise that change triggers a fear factor for some staff, particularly those who have been at a school for a long period, as teaching assistants and office staff often have been. Change brings a fear for job security; a new situation, new colleagues or a new policy can trigger anxiety or different levels of stress. Also in a time where staff restructuring has become part of the vocabulary of schools it is our teaching assistants who are going to be first in line, so their concerns are not surprising.

'Blocking' is one matter, bullying another. Some support staff, by length of service, by their standing in the community (many of them living within the catchment of the school, often as former parents at the school) act as a conduit, willingly or otherwise, for dissenting voices. A canny headteacher will recognise the influences; see the case study on page 69 and the experience of Chris Dyson. Chris has a long-standing teaching assistant who he uses as a sounding board for his changes. Such a strategy can keep a school leader grounded and in touch with how members of the school community may respond to change, as well as giving a wider sense of ownership to the decision-making process.

Bullying behaviours conducted by support staff have been identified by teachers responding to my surveys. I had several teachers who reported that teaching assistants would soon establish their 'favourites' among the newly qualified teachers each year:

> *'If you were in their gang you would have all the support you wanted: help with marking, display, little presents. But if they didn't like you they made life hell and you would be subject to rumours and gossip.'*

Others reported that details of their personal lives were known around the local community, clearly without permission, and this eventually determined the decision to leave the school. Reputational damage in the local community is close to impossible to repair.

Other teachers and also senior leaders have reported feeling undermined by support staff, particularly those adept at the art of the snide comment, disguising a criticism within a conversation but ensuring it is widely heard. Look back to page 75 at the section about how we talk to each other. A throwaway comment to one person might really get under the skin of another.

Governors

While there were no specific descriptions of the behaviour of governors as 'bullying', there were some where disquiet was expressed. Some senior leaders explained that governors were involved in what was described variously as 'personal vanity projects' or more directly as 'self-interest, of greater benefit to themselves than the school', though none added specific detail.

Other contributions were that some governors had a rather unusual view of wellbeing and that there was a concern for the mental health of the staff but not of the headteacher or deputy head. These respondents suggested that, contrary to what we will see in Chapter 4 on workload, some governors were quite happy to set tasks adding to SLT workload without specific benefit to the children and the wider school community. Though I won't quote examples here, as they might identify the schools concerned, they were often along the lines of issues that had been fully addressed at governing body meetings earlier in the year.

Of a greater level of concern to some headteachers was some governors remaining in contact with the previous incumbent. Whilst this is not an issue on a social level, from a professional perspective this is playing on a sticky wicket. A number of heads suggested that they felt quite uncomfortable at this, especially when they sensed that they were being compared to the previous regime and in some cases were being undermined. It is a difficult enough task moving into a senior leadership role in a new school and governors do need to accept that the new appointment was their decision. Whatever the strengths or otherwise of previous leaders, they have gone to pastures new and have their own concerns. However, in the more toxic schools, there is a suggestion that previous headteachers remain in contact with governors or cliques of staff often as an act of self-preservation to protect their reputations.

There were a number of headteachers who also raised concerns about governors and confidentiality. There were several who said that they felt that some governors with whom they did not have a professional relationship were using other members of staff to drip feed information back to them. This does not fall within the remit of how governors should monitor the school and most certainly undermines the wellbeing of SLT.

Challenging bullying

Never bury your head in the sand over bullying. Ignore it at the peril of the wellbeing of your staff and yourself. Nobody should fear for their job security or their mental health because of the way they are treated in the workplace. Make sure you:

- Keep your eyes and ears open. These eyes and ears could belong to other people, but tread a fine line, otherwise the culture may become one of tale telling.
- Challenge:
  - rumour and gossip
  - the way people address each other: be mindful of shaming, demeaning and intimidating language and body language

- trivial and unwarranted criticisms
- shifting goalposts and unreasonable deadlines.

- Are aware of the behaviour of your SLT and their manner, expectations and communication.
- Model empathetic behaviours with staff, children and parents, however challenging and frustrating a situation might be.
- With your middle leaders:
    - Ensure they are attuned to the culture you wish to have in the school.
    - Show no favouritism or allow any perception of it.
    - Look at the age and experience profile of your middle leadership team.
- With your support staff: communicate and keep them in the loop. Don't allow 'us and them' to develop.
- Are consistent. Nobody must think they are fireproof, whatever their role in the school. Being a long-serving stakeholder or a link to the community does not excuse any kind of behaviour.

Finally on the topic of bullying: as a leader, whether head, deputy, head of department, head of year or subject lead, consider your own actions, words and attitudes.

*

Negative or even 'toxic' cultures may arise from any of the above situations. There is a difference between poor management strategy and bullying, but to the victims of either the impact on their wellbeing is going to seem the same. SLT need to be aware of their actions, the way they are perceived and the impact they have. SLT need to lead the positive culture that will promote the mental wellbeing of their staff. However it is also the responsibility of everyone else to feed the constructive environment.

Toolkit takeaways

Develop a positive culture:

- **Be consistent.**
- **Be positive. Keep this genuine.**
- **Build relationships and grow trust.**
- **Keep calm.**

Challenge culture:

- Be visibly fair.
- Set clear communication boundaries.
- Challenge cliques and negative language.

Challenge bullying:

- Know what bullying 'looks like'.
- Be aware of your staff conduct towards each other.
- Model empathetic language and actions.
- Communicate to everyone.

PART 2

Wellbeing inaction or wellbeing in action?

4 Energising the environment: 'work' or 'workload'

Chapter overview

This chapter will consider three essential tools for our wellbeing toolkit: the reports published by the DfE in regard to reducing teacher workload.

We will consider in turn:

- planning and resourcing
- marking and feedback
- data management, assessment and reporting.

For each we will look at practical ways of addressing the issue of workload, with examples taken largely from the practice I have led at my school.

This chapter also features the discussion I had with Sean Harford about Ofsted and its impact on workload and wellbeing.

We will begin with a consideration of work and workload. We have already established that wellbeing is more than simply workload, but workload is often cited by teachers leaving the profession and by those moving schools as reasons for their departure. Workload is a frequently mentioned and hotly debated issue on teacher social media too. The DfE took the issue seriously enough to run roadshow events in the spring term of 2018 to keep workload on the agenda and to promote professional dialogue on the issue. Workload has increased through an era of greater accountability and centralised interventions assessment with the phonics screening checks in Year 1, SPAG testing (spelling, punctuation and grammar) at Key Stages 1 and 2, changes to GCSEs with Progress 8 and the future of AS levels representing a few of the changes we have seen. Change need not bring a greater workload.

Eliminating unnecessary workload

Key items in the wellbeing toolkit are the three reports published by the DfE in March 2016 addressing the reduction of teacher workload: one on planning and preparing resources, another on marking and feedback and the third on data management (DfE, 2016a, 2016b, 2016c). How many schools and teachers are aware of these? In my survey responses, 26 per cent of heads and SLT hadn't heard of them; 14 per cent were aware of them but not acting upon them; and a further small group, less than one per cent, responded very much along the lines that time and resourcing restrictions made the recommendations unworkable. The encouraging news is that 54 per cent said that they had either partly or fully implemented the suggested strategies.

In my toolkit at home I have a drill in its original box, unopened since some point in the last century and in pristine condition. It remains idle because I don't have the skills to use it without probable lasting damage to the walls, furniture or myself. If the three workload reports remain untouched in the wellbeing toolkit, is the greater cost to the school, its staff and its culture going to be in the failure to act or would damage result from rolling out the recommendations? Knock the DfE for some of its initiatives if you wish, but in terms of workload the Department is making the investment in promoting reform; the key word in the title of each report is 'eliminating' after all, closely followed by 'unnecessary', which invites reflection. The reports are a valuable resource at this time of tightening budgets and a retention and recruitment problem. In my setting, the whole staff has digested them and applied what works for us in our school.

This chapter will explore the reports in detail and I will develop further what could be put in place in terms of expectations for planning and resourcing, marking and feedback, assessments and accountability to parents. This will include examples of how we have rolled out the recommendations in my setting. I will also consider the impact upon the most precious resource teachers have: time.

Planning and resourcing

Teachers dedicate a huge amount of time to planning and resourcing their lessons. There is no getting away from planning. It needs to be done: lessons need to be prepared and resources readied for our learners. What is at issue is the extent of the planning required by the school, the time it takes, the detail required and defining what planning actually is.

Planning too often refers to daily planning of individual lessons. We can all remember our days as BEd or PGCE students and the level of detail we went to there as we learned our craft, something we may have continued into our first years in the classroom. Who is the audience of our planning though? Ultimately it is the individual teacher who will use, annotate, adapt and streamline the plan as the lesson unfolds. Many teachers, however, find that they are producing detailed plans as a response by senior leaders to a perceived demand for it from Ofsted or the DfE. Detailed planning in this way becomes almost an exercise in ticking another box on the accountability spreadsheet, adding to the workload and stress levels of teachers and senior leaders.

In one scenario, outlined in a direct message to the Healthy Toolkit Twitter account, we have a primary school where the teachers are expected to email their fully detailed plans to a member of SLT by five o'clock each Saturday evening. The plans will be returned with annotations for amendments by seven o'clock on Sunday evening. I have heard similar circumstances described both through my surveys and via social media where this expectation was raised in staff meetings where wellbeing was the key agenda item.

In these situations we have an almost complete erosion of trust, a lack of empathy, respect and mutual support, and an intrusion into the downtime of class teachers and senior leaders. Class teachers abandoned weekend plans on a regular basis to meet their Saturday deadline, whilst senior leaders spent Saturday nights and Sunday mornings dissecting the minutiae of planning documentation. In this school, some staff escaped without amendment whilst others had additions to make each week. For those who fell in between, there was the additional pressure of 'Is it good enough?' to deal with. In this particular school there was no weekend wellbeing, as planning intruded into the weekend in its entirety. The fear factor as to the consequences of not acting upon amended planning must have been near unbearable. The response of senior leaders when challenged was apparently along the lines of: 'If you don't like it, you know what to do.'

I took on the role of English leader when the National Literacy Strategy was rolled out in 1998. I devised a planning format that was a weekly overview, a single sheet of A3 with rows for each day and columns for each part of the lesson. This was in part designed with simplicity in mind, to address the new challenge of the 'Literacy Hour' and the fact that some colleagues were beginning to plan on their laptops rather than write by hand. As we all moved to electronic plans, this became a sheet for each lesson, a format retained for a number of years; it was not a million miles away from the format Ross McGill, with his Teacher Toolkit hat on, had devised in his 'Five Minute Lesson Plan', which essentially breaks down planning into what the *teacher* needs (not what SLT or Ofsted need). I shared my very simple planning format with other colleagues both in my authority and beyond. The most extraordinary feedback came from one school who told me that a teacher would have been judged 'outstanding' but hadn't written their differentiated questioning in the planning, even though it had been used in the lesson. Can we actually plan for the individual responses of every child?

Following from the previous chapter, the school with the weekend planning deadlines further illustrates the level of toxicity in some of our schools, and my anecdote shows a failure to grasp a few practicalities. When we employ new teachers, we must trust them to plan effectively and thoroughly. Nobody will go into a week in class unprepared, or underprepared, because their professionalism and their adherence to the teachers' standards determine their mindset. Yet we still hear of schools where the planning is collected each Monday morning and checked and of others where the checking is sporadic or random and teachers report high levels of anxiety in case their 'turn' arises.

The report of the independent teacher workload review group on planning and teaching resources (Department for Education, 2016c) differentiates daily planning from planning sequences of learning, which, when considering time as a factor, is a more efficient use of teacher time. Daily plans are of use to an individual teacher but may provide little more than a paper trail to satisfy any questioning about monitoring and, as the report says clearly, may only exist as an exercise in 'box-ticking' driven by the perceived demand of 'what Ofsted want', as interpreted by schools and local authorities. We can all remember the days of leaving a plan out for the headteacher during an observation; maybe you still ask for that as a leader or as a teacher you still have this requirement. Yet in carrying out an observation it is the learning, the children's books, the children's responses to the questions of the teacher and the observer that will inform the observer. Creating a detailed plan only adds more stress, particularly if it is known the lesson is going to be observed.

In my school we have made the decision to use published schemes of work, to ease the burden of planning and resourcing on our teachers. There is much high-quality material out there and it enables us to cover the curriculum fully. Schemes don't lead the teaching; the professionals take the lead and determine what will work. We don't require fully written plans but simply annotate the documents as appropriate. The teachers put their efforts in their preparation time into creating flipcharts for the interactive whiteboard and their classroom resources; this is where teachers want to be directing their energy: towards what makes a difference to the children. If teachers wish to use a planning format, which comes from force of habit, this is up to them and sight of it is not required in any monitoring. The crux of the issue with planning isn't with what is in the plan, but how it is delivered. Save time, save work, focus on the essentials and don't create unnecessary work.

Marking and feedback

Let us now turn our thoughts to the subject of marking and feedback. At some point in the last ten years some schools started asking their teachers to type out learning objective strips with steps to success, success criteria or some other related terminology. At a similar time, teachers began using green and pink highlighters to indicate whether their learning objectives had been met and also to colour code the work the children had completed. This was followed by the writing of extensive comments, often in a colour other than traditional red or blue, referring to the learning objective, the steps for success that had or had not been met, 'what went well' comments or 'even better if' statements. The children were then expected to respond to this marking at a dedicated time in the next lesson and the teachers in turn to feed back to their children in what became known as triple marking.

Does this model seem familiar? Nobody actually sets out to create additional workload for teachers, but at some point in time what began as an idea to improve marking became what was regarded as common good practice.

How this actually looked in your own schools may have differed from this representation, but I suspect that many marking policies looked very similar to this. At a similar time said policies became 'Feedback and Marking' policies, where this notion of feedback was drawn in many cases from a summary version of the work of Professor John Hattie. Hattie's work isn't a light read; how many school leaders have read the whole text? In short he emphasises the impact that well-directed feedback has on pupil learning. Hattie doesn't advocate additional work; he is an academic who suggests that effective feedback makes a difference to learning.

It is not the job of this book to address such extensive research issues. What we are going to consider is how useful marking and feedback is in terms of the workload and wellbeing of our teachers and support staff. There is no escaping the fact that, for teachers, marking has to be done, but in the context of the workload reports, which recognise that marking has become 'disproportionately valued by schools and has become unnecessarily burdensome for teachers' (Department for Education, 2016b), how much marking is enough marking, and how much of this is in the form of effective feedback?

Let's take for an example the primary school maths lesson with a multiplication focus. Each child completes a page of calculations: some get them all correct;

some make avoidable errors caused only by lack of attention; others find working accurately difficult because they don't have a firm grasp of times table facts. Would 30 individual comments be useful for the time of our colleagues? The same thought process could apply to any activity where self-marking of right or wrong answers can be used, in any subject, from pupils of any age.

Would it not be a better use of time for the children to mark their questions right or wrong and at the end of the lesson for the teacher to review the learning and to feed back in the form of three or four differentiated 'next step' tasks, written once on the whiteboard and not multiple times in books? Or do you require your teachers to place an individual feedback comment on each piece of work?

Marking and feedback grew disproportionally to the value that it provided to the pupil as school leaders perceived that Ofsted and government policy were looking for such from teachers as they responded to children's work. We had a spell, in Key Stage 2 in particular, where in responding to a piece of written work the teacher might be writing nearly as much in return. A set of books, which might take an hour to mark, would sometimes take three times as long to complete, often for children not to be able to read or understand the comment made. The marking and feedback report (Department for Education, 2016b) mentions the demoralising effect of burdensome marking expectations, the intrusion of marking into evenings and weekends, and the impact of setting next step and developmental targets. It also acknowledges as a 'myth' the notion that to be an effective teacher takes hours of marking.

'Deep marking', where the teacher gave a detailed response, often picking up on every error, before returning the work to the pupil who passed it back to the teacher for further inspection, was never an Ofsted requirement. Many teachers have reported that this was a requirement from their leaders. Responses I have had in researching this topic in my surveys, some of which are past practice but in many cases are still current, include:

- Deep marking every other piece of work, one piece of work for each group in each week or half the class at a time.
- In-depth marking of every piece of extended writing, which for a Year 6 teacher includes nearly every piece of writing.
- Marking in different colours to show positives, areas to improve and aspects for assessment.
- A given time in the next lesson to respond to the marking. This often involves reading the comment back to some children so they could understand it. With a written response to the child's comment, then marking of the next

day's work, there is little wonder that marking can feel like a hamster wheel for some teachers.

- Monitoring of books where failure to follow the policy to the letter at least resulted in a verbal warning and at worst was used in capability procedures.

This is an issue at Valance

If these excessive practices occur in the same school that has the excessive planning guidance, the wellbeing of that group of teachers is under serious threat. The marking policy becomes the elephant in the room at this point; everyone can see it but nothing is being done about it. To simply pile through the marking regardless of the impact upon one's own wellbeing will eventually impact upon physical health. I hear from teachers that their marking is monitored, but not the length of time that it takes. As a school leader, your visibility and self-awareness need to come to the fore here. Have you noticed which of your teachers are not coming to the staffroom for their lunch or at the end of school? Have you patrolled the corridors and looked in at them? If they are glued to their books and highlighters then they may be trying to get ahead, or they may find there is too much to do. Sandwich crumbs and coffee cup marks in a child's book should be a clue.

Marking as an administrative and box-ticking exercise serves little effect and time-consuming, personalised comments have little impact, as the Education Endowment Foundation makes clear in a recent report (Elliott et al., 2016). The main findings of this report were that there was a low quality of evidence about the impact of written marking and that there was a need for more studies to support teachers in developing effective marking strategies.

Time features prominently in this report, as it does in the DfE working group analysis. Remember this is our teachers' most precious resource and one that is near impossible to repay if lost. A more effective use of teacher time is to undertake some of the following suggestions, some of which we have employed at my school.

Coded communication

The use of coded communication saves time and prevents having to write lines of full sentences, which take longer to decode and understand and would be of questionable value. In our own school days we understood what a tick and cross meant after all. Our model has a little more sophistication to it:

- 'c': correction required
- 'sp': a spelling to correct
- wiggly line: grammatical problem
- inverted V: missing word

- circle: missing punctuation
- stick person: 'see an adult'.

The above is alongside a simple range of symbols understood by all adults and children.

There is a difference between mistakes and errors of understanding, which the use of symbols supports. The child making a mistake in a multiplication lesson may not need an adult to intervene. Once they realise the area for correction, the pupil can take responsibility for it and learn from it. With children who haven't grasped the concept, the teacher will need to give a different form of feedback, either by one-to-one support or a change in the level of challenge. Self-marking or peer marking of mistakes saves time – change the pen colour if you are concerned the children will change answers – and allows the teacher or teaching assistant to focus on the area of understanding. If your school insists on teacher marking of every question, the time spent on marking might cause teachers to miss that miscomprehension and a valuable opportunity. We can all learn here from PE teachers: a forward roll or dropped catch wouldn't be addressed in the next lesson. The intervention is immediate to correct or amend the action. Teaching moves on; progress, or at least consolidation, is made.

Selective or focussed marking

If everything is deep marked, your teachers will be burned out before September ends. Selective or focussed marking will benefit the pupils and save time for the teachers, allowing them a deeper understanding of the issues. Let's take our primary school class again, this time in an English lesson on the use of speech punctuation. After the initial input, children set off to work independently with two groups supported by the teacher and the teaching assistant. These two groups arguably aren't going to need in-depth marking. The high fliers, who will have 'got it' from the input, can self-mark and peer mark, as could others. There might be one group who are still getting to grips with the technical side of speech rules. It might be these six or eight children who will benefit most from the feedback given. This is not *carte blanche* for teachers to mark only half a dozen books – work and workload not being the same thing. They are still going to have an overview of the learning. Remember your value of trust!

'Return to marking'

Allowing children the time to respond to marking and teacher feedback also forms part of our workload initiative and is a reform the EEF suggested (Elliott et al., 2016). In some schools this is known as dedicated intervention and response time (DIRT) or more directly 'return to marking', and it means that the teacher feedback can be acknowledged without going down the route of extended triple marking. For both the maths and English examples from above, the teacher need write only Task 1, 2 or 3 in the books, reflecting the need to practise, consolidate or challenge. The tasks are written on the board, eliminating photocopying and sticking work in, allowing the children to complete the work at the outset of the lesson and the adults to focus their attention where the children need it.

Verbal feedback

Verbal feedback can be dismissed as 'not marking' by those with a cynical perspective but used effectively it is a timesaver for both pupils and adults. Take our speech punctuation lesson. The adults will have worked with two groups closely, supporting, scaffolding, encouraging and talking to the children about what they were doing well and what they needed to work on. Do these children, or adults, need the additional work of a written comment when they have had a double bout of teacher input? For the teacher to write 'VF' and the child to summarise what the verbal feedback was, easier at Key Stage 2 and beyond to be fair, gives the child ownership and requires only teacher or teaching assistant acknowledgement by initial or stamper.

The time implications of a sensible feedback and marking policy are that marking does not become an unnecessary burden and at the same time it is useful to supporting the progress of our learners. Built into the regular monitoring cycle and reviewed termly as a whole staff, it will gradually become ingrained as a habit of good teaching as well as reflecting the culture of support of, trust in and respect for the professionalism of our teaching staff.

Data management, assessment and reporting

The data management report (Department for Education, 2016a) is explicit in its opening summary that school leaders should challenge themselves to identify what data is useful and what purpose it will serve and then to collect the minimum amount of data to evaluate what they are doing: 'collect once, use many times', be ruthless, be prepared to say no to something that is being done because it has always been this way and think about workload. Of the three reports, this is the one that is the most blunt when it relates to workload, referring to data collection causing increasing workload for teachers and leaders without discernible benefit, stating explicitly that schools should be able to have greater freedom to balance professional autonomy against the demands of the accountability system.

According to the report, 56 per cent of respondents to the DfE Workload Challenge survey reported that they felt the workload related to assessment was too high, something which had developed historically through the era of levels, sub-levels, non-statutory testing, assessment for learning (AfL), assessing pupil progress (APP) and any other number of changes and initiatives. A key turning point came with assessment without levels, when schools and many of the commercial assessment providers, without a clear picture of what was happening with assessment, transferred their old framework to the new one with a massive impact on data workload, so that not only were schools getting their heads around a new curriculum, their teachers were also faced with an often unwieldy online system with an expectation of tracking every objective for every child.

The core message of the DfE report on data management is 'less is more' and that the focus should be on making sure teachers know their children. Assessing against key performance indicators in the core subjects, working with standardised tests and knowing that Ofsted don't want a particular format for assessment are reassuring messages. Another, found on page 8 of the report, aligns with the message of *The Wellbeing Toolkit*: data management should support the values and ethos of the school.

So how do we unpack the values from our toolkit to support assessment and data management? Several values are significant here. Have empathy for what your teachers have to do. If that spreadsheet takes an age to fill in, can you ditch it? Respect their professional judgements and support their judgements with the expertise of colleagues both within and outside your establishment. Most of all, give your teachers time to adjust to any change and plenty of notice of deadlines because a last-minute panic is going to stress your teachers and you.

In my school we did away with recording formative assessment. I am aware of planning formats that include an AfL grid along the bottom of the document with the children's names and objectives for the lesson. Ten lessons a week in English and maths, 30 children, two or three objectives for each lesson equals 600–900 assessments, and that says all you need to know. Who is going to check this? Formative assessment is only of use to the teacher and they are going to do their own if you are a leader who trusts your staff and respects their judgements. A good teacher will know their children without having to record the minutiae of each lesson.

We stopped doing six data drops a year in favour of three, and we used a common model for reading and writing with a standardised score, which two years on is understood by the teachers. They send me the data on a spreadsheet, I do the calculations of progress and colour coding of attainment, and this forms the basis of dialogue for pupil progress. Tests aren't everything, but they are an additional perspective to a rounder understanding of a child and their attainment.

We took the assessment report and the principles behind it one step further in our written reports, an area which has had a major positive impact upon our teacher workload and wellbeing.

End-of-year reports

The written report is one of those requirements that schools are obliged to provide. Primary teachers in particular will know the experience of spending the entire May half term writing and editing reports. Some of these are still substantial in length and complexity.

The most burdensome report I have been made aware of is A3 sized, with text boxes for each subject, densely written in full prose with a personal and differentiated comment for each child in each subject, with a back page detailing assessment scores, targets for the next year, followed by a detailed class teacher comment and the headteacher's sign off. 2,000 words per child times 30; you do the maths, but that is approximately the word count of this book. Each took up to two hours to type. Add this report burden to the existing workload in the summer term: end-of-year assessments, statutory testing, maybe an inspection. Writing reports is an absolute deadline too; there can be no excuse for not getting these to the parents in time.

The burden is no less for secondary teachers either. Writing for one subject alone may have benefits in one way, but if working with up to ten classes then the overall word count will be similar to the primary reports. Furthermore, someone, a form tutor or a colleague in an administration role, has to coordinate and correlate the reports, chase missing ones and ensure the records are complete.

Is there any easing of this burden? Though the workload reports do not mention report writing specifically, the principles they each employ can be applied here. Namely, what is necessary and is it creating additional workload?

Take the primary school report that reports on every subject. In many primary schools there will be an overview of the term's work sent to parents three times a year. Let's take history, for example: the parents might be told that the children are studying a Victorian childhood, local history and the Ancient Greeks. More often than not, the end-of-year report will tell the very same parents that these three areas have been studied. Why? They know this because they have been told already, probably helped with a Victorian school costume, found a few local landmarks and maybe built a model Parthenon out of cardboard tubes with their child. Having also discussed this on parents' evenings with the class teacher, they are well aware of what their child has done. Therefore repeating the same comment on 30 reports is duplicating something that has already been said and of no useful purpose.

A few readers will recall having to handwrite reports, with a duplicate on pink paper underneath. Now everything is word processed, the teacher's best friends are 'cut and paste' and the thesaurus tool. Teachers have reported being asked to change reports because they were too similar. Transposing 'he' and 'she', 'him' and 'her' is a common error and copying another child's name a little careless, but these aside, does a similar or identical comment matter that much for two children of a similar ability when trying to condense a year's work into four lines? Which parents are reading other children's reports (excluding those with twins, of course)? Parents might compare reports but so long as the information given is accurate and the communication with the school is good, why create an extra level of workload?

Parents are always pleased to receive the end-of-year report at primary school but almost without exception the first part they turn to is the teacher and headteacher comments, which are the only completely personal part of the report. Then they will look at the results. For parents these are the most important parts of the school report, because they are informed about the progress their child has made.

Do current school reports make efficient use of teacher time? Do they add to teacher workload and are they fit for purpose?

With these questions and previous considerations in this section in mind, we redesigned the reports at my school in quite a radical overhaul, which has considerably reduced the burden on teachers. The first step was to literally cut them in half; there isn't one report but two and no extra work to go with it. One is written in spring, the other in summer, but both together cover the statutory requirement to report to parents.

The spring term report begins with a simple grid of behaviours for learning marked off on a one-to-five scale (see Table 4.1). The same grid is repeated in the summer term for a simple comparison for teacher and parents. Simple and informative, the act of putting a cross in a box saves writing 'Jasmine is able to concentrate for short periods without adult intervention', or a variation on this, 30 times.

There follows a section for reading, writing and mathematics, written in the traditional prose format with a limit of ten lines and a fixed font size of 12 (see Table 4.2).

The targets are for the remaining part of the school year, and relate to key skills and concepts. Setting targets in spring is an essential part of our teacher wellbeing and workload consideration. To set them halfway through the year gives the child and the teacher a sense of ownership. Setting them in July may be of little relevance to the new teacher in September.

Table 4.1: Example behaviours for learning grid

	1 Unsatisfactory	2 Requires improvement	3 Satisfactory	4 Good	5 Excellent
Perseverance in lessons					
Focus and concentration					
Independence					
Social skills					
Behaviour and manners					

Table 4.2: Example written section for mathematics

Mathematics
Targets in mathematics: • To... • To... • To...

The summer report has the same behaviours grid as referenced above and also lists effort in each subject on the same one-to-five scale. This scale is also used to show progress for reading, writing and mathematics. Attainment for all subjects is listed in terms of working below (BLW), working towards (WTS), working at (EXS) or working above (GDS) the age-related standard. See Tables 4.3 and 4.4 for examples.

There then follows the only prose, which is the teacher comment. This allows for reflection on the targets and learning in general, followed by a headteacher comment box. Each document is to be a strict A4 sheet only with no reduction in font size permitted, as this would create more work in filling the space.

The impact on our teachers' workload has been substantial. The thinking behind the spring term report is that if teachers were to spend half term writing reports they would rather do it in February when it is dark, wet and cold and there is less inclination to go out than in the May break with its bank holiday and long, warm

Table 4.3: Example report on reading, writing and mathematics

Subject	Effort	Progress	Attainment
Reading	5	4	GDS
Writing	5	4	EXS
Mathematics	5	3	EXS

Table 4.4: Example report on the foundation subjects

Subject	Effort	Attainment
Science	5	EXS
Computing	5	EXS
History	5	GDS
Geography	5	GDS
Art	5	EXS
Design and technology	5	EXS
Modern foreign languages	4	EXS
Music	5	EXS
Religious education	5	EXS
PSHE	4	EXS
PE	4	EXS

evenings. This doesn't mean they are expected to spend all of the week working. The template goes out just after Christmas and we encourage the first six reports to be done at least a week before the break. We have managed some report release time in the last year or two, but budget cuts are squeezing that a little now. The deadline is the week after half term when the reports are sent home, but the other crucial workload decision was that this report is used as a point to discuss the child's progress at parents' evening, which is scheduled for the following week.

Summer is where the real difference has been noticed because the prose has been cut and the teachers have the time to make a really personal and reflective comment on the child. To save time for teachers and senior leaders, there are three deadlines instead of one: for the first six and then for two batches of 12, allowing up to five weeks for completion. Over the last year or two, to see the Twitter traffic of teachers sharing their angst about the number of reports they had done each day during and after half term showed me just how far we had come in our report writing schedule.

How could schools implement something similar? We give our teachers the templates for reports early in the year so they can at the very least enter each child's name and save a file for each child. To support their workload, we suggested a schedule of spreading the load, aiming for six a week (in both spring and summer term), which helped senior leaders in proofreading and adding final comments. For a time, before the budget became a little tighter, we were able to grant teachers some additional hours to write reports in school time. Due to how concise the reports were, many colleagues found they were able to write ten or more reports in a week and be ready well ahead of schedule.

Simple tweaking of the diary and timetable is all that is required.

Ofsted and workload

Sean Harford knows what it is like on the other side of the inspector's clipboard. Before being appointed to the inspectorate, he was a successful science teacher and senior leader in a school in the east of England and since September 2015 has served as National Director, Education at Ofsted. In that time he has embraced social media to build transparency and perhaps in a bid to reduce the fear factor around the inspection regime, something he has continued to do through his appearances at events for school leaders.

At the end of August 2017, as schools in England and Wales prepared to return for the new academic year, Sean tweeted (Harford, 2017a), in an effort to promote positive thinking: 'Okay #SLT what's one thing you'll pledge to do to reduce your teachers' workload in the coming new year?' This raised several responses, including: 'Best thing #SLT can do is not waste teacher time in long meetings, setting unplanned deadlines or time-consuming tasks with little meaning', themes we have already explored in some depth.

In his Ofsted blog a few days later (Harford, 2017b), Sean acknowledged that there were some negative responses, which, given the inspectorate's history and the often adversarial nature of Twitter, was not to be unexpected. Many of the replies had, however, given Sean an indication that some senior leaders were taking workload seriously. As a result, the following question was added to the survey that school staff take during an inspection: 'Leaders and managers take workload into account when developing and implementing policies and procedures so as to avoid placing unnecessary burdens on staff', with space to add further comment in a free text box at the end.

It would be a challenge for Ofsted inspectors to 'judge' the culture of an establishment, but they are able to gain an approximation of it from what they see, hear and ask, and how the children learn and develop. Though inspections can be rigorous, if not bruising, experiences, inspectors, like it or not, are adept at identifying key indicators that highlight aspects of school culture.

Likewise with staff wellbeing, whilst not commenting upon it as such, inspectors would be able to see from the staff survey if there were concerns to pick up on and investigate further. One such concern might be the consideration SLT put towards workload when introducing new initiatives. Sean agrees with the principle that where introducing a new initiative, something else should be dropped from the requirements that teachers otherwise have. He would like to see an ethos of trust in schools, trust to experiment with practice and policies. Whether schools who have been on the sharp end of a tough inspection would feel the same is a moot point, but the core message of trust, where trust is embedded in the school culture, should be recognised.

Sean recognises that the fear of Ofsted and the inspection process adds to the anxiety of senior leaders and of teachers and hence to a negative impact on their wellbeing. Previous chief inspectors with a more fractured relationship with the profession may have contributed to this feeling. However, Sean firmly believes that calls for the abolition of the inspectorate, as the National Education Union (Hazell, 2018) and the Liberal Democrats (George, 2018) both advocate, are misguided. Sean is also very firm in his belief that 'Mocksteds' should not be taking place; they are an additional burden on schools and can trigger fear and anxiety among staff who still take the myths about inspection as the gospel truth, fear perhaps greater than in an official inspection.

Like most other publicly funded bodies, Ofsted has also been subject to reduced budgets and an impact upon the workload of its employees, with nine out of 12 inspectors with two years' or less service leaving the watchdog citing workload among their reasons for moving on (Roberts, 2018). Though it may not come as a comfort to some schools, Ofsted has a retention and recruitment issue too.

How though does Ofsted try to alleviate or minimise the impact it has on our workload and wellbeing? First, we need to take a look at their myth-busting document (Ofsted, 2018), which, although it has its fair share of cynical critics on social media, does seek to counter all those 'Ofsted want to see this' comments that are so often repeated on social media or at local leaders' meetings. There are some statements in this document, specifically related to workload, that are worth reproducing here to remind school leaders what your wellbeing toolkit needs to contain.

On lesson planning

Does planning need to be micromanaged for our teachers who clearly can plan for great learning experiences without churning out reams of Word documents? Ofsted say no:

Ofsted does not require schools to provide individual lesson plans to inspectors [...] Inspectors are interested in the effectiveness of planning rather than the form it takes.'

If we reverse 'Ofsted want to see...' to 'Ofsted don't want to see...' in our language and also in our practice, we can begin to lighten the pressure on our teachers. We must take on board the second point in the way we work too. Ofsted are clearly aware of the burden planning takes. Setting it out in a grid, using the 'right' font and colour-coded plans – if it doesn't benefit the way we teach the children, there is no place for it in the school.

On lesson grading and lesson observation

There are still schools that grade lessons despite formal grading having been off the agenda of the inspectorate for some years. Why are we still grading then? Don't we trust our teachers to perform week in week out? Or is it to exercise a degree of control, a reminder of who is the boss?

Inspectors do not grade individual lessons. Ofsted does not expect schools to use the Ofsted evaluation schedule to grade teaching or individual lessons. [...] Ofsted does not require schools to undertake a specified amount of lesson observation.'

This can be no clearer. Formal lesson grading is not required. This does not mean that areas for concern can't be addressed through professional dialogue, but it does mean the continual striving for 'outstanding' doesn't need to appear in that conversation.

On pupils' work and evidence for inspection

Marking policies, however burdensome they are, do not have to satisfy the inspectors. There just needs to be a correlation between the policy and the marking they see:

> *Ofsted does not expect to see any specific frequency, type or volume of marking and feedback; these are for the school to decide through its assessment policy. [...] Ofsted does not expect to see any written record of oral feedback provided to pupils by teachers.'*

This reinforces the need not to record formative assessment, as discussed on page 108; if Ofsted don't need it, then why do it?

> *Ofsted does not require teachers to undertake additional work or to ask pupils to undertake work specifically for the inspection.'*

Undertaking additional work is one of the enemies of wellbeing. When I met Sean, and having heard him speak a few days before, he reiterated a core principle: if we ask teachers to do something new or different, we should be taking something away in return.

I promised Sean a quote in *The Wellbeing Toolkit*, so returning to his days at the chalkface he left me with this thought about workload:

> *Workload is workload if you are told what to do; if you want to do something, and you are really interested in it and passionate about it, then you don't see it as workload.'*

*

The DfE has produced three laudable and well-intentioned reports addressing workload around planning, marking and data management. Although there were some raised eyebrows on social media about a decision to launch their own 'toolkit' on the first weekend of the summer holiday for English schools in 2018, in the long run the Department has delivered advice on the reduction of workload. Nevertheless, the responsibility to deliver this lies with the leaders of our individual schools and our MATs and the adoption of workable, sensible and principled policies to eradicate tasks that have little measurable impact on pupil outcomes, stop our teachers working efficiently and cause them needless stress. Ultimately this relies on the school growing the culture and values needed to care for their staff.

Toolkit takeaways

Never allow 'work' and 'workload' to be confused. Work can't go away, but unnecessary work can. If it isn't having an impact on the children and their

learning then eliminate it, and for everything new you ask your teachers to do, take something equivalent away.

Planning:

- Trust your teachers. Don't require the submission of lesson plans by email, don't call in plans each week for monitoring and don't call for them at no notice.
- Keep plans simple and avoid unnecessary printing.
- Use planning sequences and commercially available and proven plans, and allow annotation. Cutting and pasting into a school format is a waste of time, effort and paper.

Feedback and marking:

- Ask yourself:
  - Is your current marking actually having any impact on the learning?
  - Is your marking eroding teacher time? Are your teachers sitting in their rooms during lunch and for hours after school and taking marking home?
  - Is marking merely a tick-box exercise?
- Consider codes and symbols for simplicity of communication and to save time.
- Use self-marking and peer marking to save time and enhance pupil understanding.
- Use selective marking and feedback for identified groups and individuals and for core aspects of learning.
- Use verbal feedback with pupil responses to it.

Data, assessment and reporting:

- Keep to three data drops a year.
- Use your data, reuse it and analyse it, but never ask for it to be repeated.
- When writing reports:
  - Be precise.
  - Be concise.
  - Don't repeat what parents already know.
  - Use them as a discussion point with parents.
  - Split the workload: spring term reports are the future.
  - Grids and grades are easier and more precise than prose.
  - Let your teachers and pupils 'own' their targets.

Ofsted:

- Read the Ofsted myth-busting document and in particular what it says about planning, grading, lesson observation and the children's work.
- Do not hold 'Mocksteds'. They are a waste of time and money and an unnecessary strain on the mental wellbeing of the whole staff.

---

5 Career satisfaction

Chapter overview

This chapter discusses the challenge of providing career satisfaction within a wellbeing context. We will cover:

- **The nature of career progression and the challenges to it in our current environment, bearing in mind school cultures, the opportunities to progress and the challenges that school location presents.**
- **Performance management and how ineffectual or unforgiving appraisal processes can be modelled into an effective experience through the use of a coaching approach.**

Think back to the people you have encountered in your teaching career, to those you trained with and your first colleagues. Are they still in teaching in some form or other: in class, leadership, inspecting or consulting? How about the people you encountered along the way – those who became friends, those who were passing acquaintances, those you were on nodding terms with, or that lady or gentleman nobody knew very much about?

They leave teaching for a variety of reasons. Maybe they have retired or have left because of a change in family or personal circumstances. A number will set out with a five- or ten-year plan before doing something different. Some of these teachers may return in some way; others may never give it a second thought. For all those who left teaching with a degree of self-management of their future, there were also those who could not exercise this control. A minority will have departed because of questions over their suitability to teach. A number will have faced redundancy (on the increase in the current climate), some will have taken early retirement, but others will have quit the profession because of workload, bullying or being pushed out of their role.

It is of this last group that we can question their career satisfaction. In theory our teachers will work for up to 40 years. For every person who has the boundless enthusiasm to proclaim on social media their joys at the beginning of the school year, there will be those who don't and won't share their multicoloured displays, newly discovered gems in reading or their foolproof guide to never marking another book. For those who do share, ask yourselves whether in ten years it will be the same or whether their enthusiasm will wane with the passage of time and whether cynicism will overtake youthful exuberance.

Teaching is a wearing occupation. There are few other professions requiring degree-level entry with such capacity to exhaust, physically and mentally, or with such dropout rates. Some students don't make it out of initial training; in my 1992 PGCE cohort around five per cent never made it into a position at the end of the year. In more recent scenarios, dropout rates in the first years of different routes into the job are hugely variable. Those trained as part of Teach First, for example, have a retention rate of 80 per cent after one year but only 43 per cent after three years (Scott, 2016).

In 2013, it seemed that 'teachers [were] the happiest workers in Britain', or so proclaimed the *Telegraph* (Hall, 2013), but the BBC in the same year didn't agree (BBC, 2013), saying teachers were 'increasingly dissatisfied', and four years later the *Guardian* told us that even cutting workload wasn't stopping teachers from leaving (Scutt, 2017). Whether the surveys cited in these articles asked leading questions is not for consideration here but there are two practical aspects we have yet to cover in relation to wellbeing for school staff: the practical opportunity for career progression and the impact of performance management.

Career progression is an important part of our holistic approach to wellbeing. As leaders we mustn't think in terms of mere bodies in front of classes, because these bodies are the ones who deliver good teaching and learning, inspire our young people and continue to build our positive school culture.

Moving on up... or moving on out

We have covered school culture and bullying in some depth, alongside workload and whether reforms have been enacted or ignored, but all of these elements also have an impact on career progression.

Does the culture of the school allow for fair career progression? If the school uses performance management effectively to support professional development, then it may well be fair, but if the culture is one of catching colleagues out or working to a tick list, teachers may feel otherwise.

Is the capacity or willingness of our teachers to accept more in the way of workload influencing their chances for promotion and career development? In schools where workload isn't being addressed, where there are high levels of scrutiny and where 'Ofsted want to see this' is the mantra, then staying in post might mean taking on the workload just to secure career progression.

How much is geography a consideration for teacher progression and wellbeing? More than can be imagined.

For a teacher based in London, if they are unhappy in one school there is sufficient choice for an alternative post. There are 32 boroughs, some with a number of MATs and some with none, a smattering of free schools and reasonably reliable public transport. This could mean that a young teacher could begin in one school and, in theory, change jobs each summer for their whole career. Most don't of course, but I have known several teachers who serve a three- to four-year stint in a school before moving on, often to a promoted post. There is a problem in retaining teachers in London, however, principally because of the cost of living. A young teacher might be tempted by the capital and its bright lights, but rental costs are high and purchasing a property on one teacher salary alone is very difficult.

Other parts of the country are slightly more affordable if not as accessible. I grew up in the north-west of England and at both primary and secondary school all our student teachers on placement were from the local teacher training institution, many of them staying on in their first teaching role. There are good road links, two thriving cities in Liverpool and Manchester and enough access to culture, entertainment and sport to satisfy the tastes of a young teacher relocating to begin their first post. This would be equally true of other large metropolitan areas.

There are coastal towns, particularly on the east coast, that are more remote and that don't have the attractions to tempt teachers to move. Areas of Scotland too cannot rely upon the beauty of their surroundings alone to recruit new staff. Schools in every area of the country have recruitment and retention challenges determined by their individual geographical context.

The wellbeing challenge for all schools, however, is two-fold: firstly in looking after their teachers in the ways *The Wellbeing Toolkit* has already set out and secondly in giving teachers the opportunity to progress, to have that career satisfaction that will retain them in the profession. This is no easy test to overcome, as in a small town with a limited number of schools the options for sideways moves are restricted unless the teacher is prepared to relocate or to commute.

Teachers may seek to move schools for any number of reasons: for challenge, for career progression, for relocation, amongst others. Whilst there are positions in other schools, particularly in subject areas where there are shortages, other considerations come into play. Teachers may not be able to move because of family circumstances; childcare issues or elderly parents may be keeping them where they are. The potential stress of renting, buying or selling a property, just to move schools, may also be holding them back. Equally, there are the teachers who have found it impossible to move, their paths blocked by the lack of promotion opportunities or by a challenging environment, without a post to go to. It takes a brave person to take the leap of faith to leave a school without another position to go to and to rely upon their abilities to win a new role or trust in the supply agencies to find them further opportunities.

Where there are few other schools for teachers to move to, or to recruit from, the onus is on the school to build a nurturing and supportive environment to retain teachers. Knowing that recruiting teachers from beyond a reasonable distance is going to be difficult enough, there needs to be an environment where teachers can feel they can progress their careers in ways other than waiting to fill the shoes of a retiree. Working in a federation or a MAT can allow opportunities to share expertise beyond one school, allowing a teacher to build their professional reputation.

Being in a stand-alone school doesn't preclude the building of links with others. For the science leader who has developed an innovative way of leading whole-class investigations, to share this with other primaries is an extra string to the bow and a professional challenge that working within their own school doesn't allow. For the PE department, to allow less experienced teachers to link with the primaries that provide their Year 7 intake gives the opportunity to cascade their expertise and skill to primary staff and children alike. While such practice won't be unfamiliar to schools in terms of professional development, within the wider context of wellbeing and career satisfaction, this is an area to bear in mind for retaining staff as much as recruiting them.

Give your staff every opportunity to seek continued professional development. Invest some time in looking for courses that support not only subject knowledge but professionalism too. Leadership courses, especially with an empathy focus, coaching, effective observation and appraisal can add to our expertise but also, used appropriately, actively promote wellbeing, as we will discover on page 125.

Performance management: a circus or a bear pit?

Executed properly, the cycle of performance management allows our teachers and other staff, at whatever stage of their career, to consolidate their development and find new themes and aspects of education to move into. Poorly delivered, it veers between utterly pointless and a poisoned chalice. Appraisal of staff has to be completed, which makes us no different from other professions, but in terms of staff wellbeing I believe that we are missing an opportunity to use appraisals to improve career satisfaction and retain our teachers. In analysing my survey answers on performance management, it became apparent that appraisal falls into one of three broad categories: effective, ineffectual and unforgiving.

Ineffectual appraisal

Here we are back with the tick-box attitude. Performance management is done because it has to be but there is little enthusiasm for the process. The bare minimum of targets and little, if any, development of practice characterised this category of responses. This serves little purpose and in truth for both parties is a waste of time, our most precious resource.

Typical responses indicated that the cycle in many cases wasn't completed, interim observations and meetings falling by the wayside because of staff illness or cover issues. Some reported that the final meeting never took place and they were simply given the paperwork to sign, in some cases more than a year late, with no feedback.

This anxious delay to the receipt of feedback can compromise wellbeing and it is hardly celebrating achievement or showing respect for the work a teacher does either. While completing the cycle to move up the pay scale is one matter, once at the top of it, the ineffectual approach represents no satisfaction at all.

Unforgiving appraisal

Whilst the ineffectual approach sees the cycle as just another task to complete, the unforgiving tactic takes us back to the toxic side of school culture: overbearing, pedantic and in some cases malevolent.

The worst cases are those with such a multitude of targets that the performance management documentation becomes the sole attribute of teaching, rather than a mere part of it. Teaching cannot be summed up in three, five or even 20 targets – the most extreme figure I heard of. It is far more complex than this as we know with planning, marking, assessing, behaviour management, classroom organisation, targets, progress and reports; this list barely scratches the surface. Yet the unforgiving appraiser with highly specific targets in a highly pressured environment effectively makes the focus entirely upon results. While nobody would dismiss the importance of excellent teaching and pupils working to the best of their ability, if your teachers' focus is only on what is in the appraisal document wider issues such as social skills and pupil wellbeing are going to be of low or no priority.

Targets that list specific aspects to be seen in observations, books and marking (in an extreme case of micromanagement) as good as dictate to the teacher what should be seen and effectively show no trust or respect for teacher independence and professional ability. There is a colossal difference between targets set for a teacher who needs support and those set for one with whom there are no concerns. Even with a teacher who is struggling, targets need to be set so they are supportive and coach them through the process of improvement, not be put in place to catch them out and trigger capability proceedings. For the teacher who is more than competent, the use of performance management with excessive targets serves little purpose, unless the intention is to marginalise, bully or manage someone out of school.

Teachers being told that their 'head would be on the block' if certain results weren't achieved, observed under difficult circumstances at little notice or given feedback riven with negative comments and little constructive conversation are going to have heightened anxiety, feel pressured and be unlikely to perform well. When teachers have their appraisal passed to others, the possibilities of exposure to a more hostile environment are too obvious. As we identified in Chapter 3, page 65, the potential for those who take their stresses out upon others or who take the term 'leader' to mean 'throwing one's weight around' can expose less experienced staff to unfair and unprofessional treatment. The observation of a lesson by someone without training or experience in what to look for, or armed with a tick sheet containing ill-defined terminology on lesson content, invites negativity and uninformed criticism. Little wonder then that some teachers describe their experience of such toxicity as 'like post-traumatic stress.'

Somebody's watching me: a word on observation

Though many schools have now cast aside grading lessons, there still remains an active subculture of how to create the perfect lesson. As a school leader, I am sure you can see through the 'performance' lesson, which in some cases has been 'rehearsed' beforehand. More effective and more informative observation comes from unannounced observation, though there is a wellbeing consideration here. A number of my surveys indicated a level of stress at unannounced learning walks with no feedback. The answer here is twofold: firstly give plenty of notice that, for example, in the fourth week of term there will be a learning walk looking at the teaching of mathematics; secondly, make your class visits a regular event as part of your visible leadership. Dropping by is a powerful way of building relationships with the children, who otherwise may only see a leader in an office. It also shows your staff that you have a handle on what is going on in the school. Both these approaches will enable trust to be built and a level of confidence on the part of your teachers who will not feel under the microscope in such a positive culture.

Effective appraisal

The best cycles of performance management allow for a sound professional conversation through the course of the entire year and beyond. Supportive leaders allow their colleagues to bring their own professional development needs to the initial meeting and individual as well as whole-school focussed targets can ensue. They incorporate a full understanding of the needs of the children in the class, allow for sufficient challenge whilst acknowledging the reality that a classroom may not be a perfectly organised and disciplined place at all times, but that the professional integrity of teachers is respected and celebrated. Observations become an opportunity to reflect on teaching and learning in practice, areas for personal development and the use of technology and resources in the classroom.

What effective appraisal looks like

Think about context

How good are you at appraisal? Is it regarded as a dull, routine activity that people shy away from or is it more vibrant? Even though the school may say that performance appraisals are important, ensure the process is taken seriously.

Assess your attitude towards the process

Don't go through your appraisal just for the sake of it. Consider what the value of the process is to both parties. An appraisal gives colleagues many opportunities to plan what they want to do next in their work, so grasp those opportunities with both hands.

Encourage staff to make a wish list

What do they want from their performance appraisal? A map of their future career or future stability? Ask what opportunities to learn and develop they wish to have.

Make sure it happens

Both parties must insist appraisal takes place and staff must be able to challenge you if it doesn't.

Prepare

Preparing for the appraisal is vital. Both sides should gather relevant information – particularly anything that shows objectives have been met. Encourage staff to keep a diary or file of their achievements. Let your staff be really clear about what they want out of the discussion and encourage them to take along examples of their work and feedback from other colleagues.

Follow up

Keep accurate notes and share them with the member of staff as soon as possible, so no ambiguity or confusion arises.

Keep your promises

This is part of the ongoing support and development of your staff. You want your staff to succeed and this one formal process is excellent for emphasising this.

Give feedback regularly

Life never stays static, so it's important to make sure your feedback is regular, even outside of the formal appraisal process.

In short, everyone benefits: the school, the pupils and crucially our teaching colleagues and teaching assistants. Even for those at the top of their pay spine, the satisfaction is there because it develops skills, builds professional prestige and adds suitable experience for when the time comes to look for promotion. The coaching approach here is the crucial tool in the toolkit.

*

This chapter essentially explores how our professional conversation addresses wellbeing beyond the issues of workload and incorporating our continued professional development. Without career satisfaction the career becomes merely a job with no guarantee of longevity for the teacher, the school and education as a whole. Within the holistic definition of wellbeing, providing the best support for your teachers in the academic and geographical context of the school, alongside a principled and authentic appraisal cycle, will give you a further vital piece of your toolkit.

Toolkit takeaways

- Be aware of your school context: one size doesn't fit all:
  - Your location could be key to retention. If you are the only school for miles around then plan carefully how to retain your staff.
  - Provide opportunities to share and model expertise to grow the leadership opportunities available.
  - Don't let teachers go 'stale', as working for years with the same year group or timetable isn't going to encourage reflection and improvement.
- Be aware of those who don't move on despite poor relationships with colleagues. If they can't leave, for family commitments for example, ensure they are looked after and protected from a toxic environment and any bullying.
- Think about professional development opportunities laterally rather than in a linear fashion. How far can your teachers benefit others as well as develop themselves?
- Make performance management count:
  - Coaching-led appraisal generates good professional conversation and benefits all sides.
  - Match your appraisers with staff thoughtfully for professional development of both parties.
  - Tokenistic application benefits nobody.
  - Appraisal delivered with ill intent or to add weight to workload will drive staff away – to other schools, out of the profession or to ill health caused by stress and anxiety. Your teachers' mental health is as much your responsibility as their own.

6 Work–life balance and healthy attitudes

Chapter overview

In this chapter we will discuss what work–life balance actually means to teachers in the current environment and what they consider their priorities to be, before developing how school leaders can actively promote an effective culture and model of work–life balance as part of their wellbeing toolkit.

Thinking of work–life balance over the whole calendar year, we will also cover how school life has, in some cases, impacted upon the holiday time of our teachers and the ways such intrusion can be avoided.

There is no one clear definition of what work–life balance is. Quite simply that is because it differs for everyone, because we are also diverse in our lives, life choices and personalities. For our friends and loved ones working to shift patterns and fixed hours and without the intrusion of their work into evenings and weekends, any discussion about work–life balance is going to be alien. However for school staff, teachers in particular, the issue of juggling their work and life commitments is one that is constantly under their own scrutiny and pressured by the circumstances in their workplace.

Consider your wellbeing offer to your staff. It probably mentions 'work–life balance' in there somewhere. It may even say it is an entitlement but it is probably unlikely to define it. This chapter aims to help school leaders at least facilitate work–life balance as an attainable target for teachers.

The staff wellbeing survey

Use your staff wellbeing survey to ask staff to define work–life balance in their terms and in their context. A text box with a few lines will allow for some depth of answers. Some reference to the broad definitions in this chapter may also help colleagues in their definition. When analysing the results of your survey, look for:

- **Trends:** What do people want and how can you support this without intruding?
- **Potential actions:** What can you cut out, reduce or delegate to support work–life balance?
- **Potential outcomes:** What can you do that will make a tangible difference: a measured unit of time or an actual reduction in work taken off site?

Work, rest and play?

A general definition of work–life balance is that work time and personal life should be complementary rather than competing priorities. In commerce and industry, many employers will adopt family-friendly policies. These will be in place not only for retention, recruitment and employee satisfaction but also to promote productivity. Our 'productivity' in schools is defined by our examination results and our Ofsted grading, which is a compelling case to ensure our teachers have the work–life balance they need.

Through Twitter I asked teachers to define what work–life balance meant to them. To make our wellbeing offer meaningful we need to consider the variety of meanings that this holds to UK teachers. Responses fell into several broad categories: enjoyment, family time, organising time and doing 'the important stuff'.

Enjoyment

Echoing the themes of the previous chapter, one tweeter said that work–life balance meant that everything they had to do felt manageable and that they were able to enjoy it, so that 'I positively anticipate what I have in store rather than feel drained at the thought of it.' If there was to be a broad definition of work–life balance, this would be a good starting point. The crucial words here are 'manageable' and 'enjoy', and if we enable our staff to do both through our principled approach, we are making a decent start.

Among the responses were the importance of time for film and theatre, and watching and playing sport, how 'work, rest and play are big parts of my life', feeling comfortable with life choices and not being made to feel guilty about doing so.

Another response was 'Love, laughter and letting go!', which emphasises the importance of having a happy team and not letting the pressure, negativity and triviality erode the resilience of our colleagues. Taking anxiety and stress home and taking these out on loved ones is not an indicator of a contented colleague.

Family time

One reply described teaching before parenthood as a hobby, working an uninterrupted 12-hour day but ensuring the weekends and evenings were hers, but now it was about being able to spend time at work and alone 'without the mum guilt!' To many the concept of working 12 hours straight may not appeal, but it was this teacher's choice and she was able to manage her work–life balance to suit her. Several others mentioned the precious time spent with their own children and partners.

Work–life balance changes with parenthood, as does the attitude of others, as we will explore further in Chapter 7, page 147.

Organising time

Several colleagues referred to leaving both the physical and mental workload behind at school. Some teachers will choose to complete all their marking and preparation in school time, whilst others will choose to take work home. This suits them and their organisation. It is not for the school to check the arrival and departure times of their teachers and be judgemental about this.

Many others discussed how having control and making their own choices about workload were important, where and when they worked and how they did it. If our staff have the confidence to say that workload isn't benefiting them and is impacting negatively upon other aspects of life, then we send one precise wellbeing message. Acknowledging and then acting upon this are the next most vital steps.

'If I'm tired, I sleep; if I'm ill, I rest; and if my friends are around, I socialise' were the words of another colleague who further added the absolute importance of 'me time' to their own agenda. Another talked of clocking in and out at the same time every day and not checking school email once away from the premises, whilst acknowledging that they were guilty of not following this all the time.

When we take on newly qualified staff in our schools, we can forget that they don't have the experience to say that the 'to-do list' can sometimes wait and parts of it can be omitted. This is worthy of some serious consideration to avoid cases of early burnout.

Doing 'the important stuff'

One of the most detailed responses talked of enjoying the company of 'people who love and hear me when I'm not talking', as well as those who made this teacher laugh, offered them a challenge and gave them the opportunity to be themselves. This colleague very much emphasised the importance of relationships both within and outside school. If the balance tips too much to the work side, relationships with friends and partners are in danger of being compromised.

A different reply suggested 'work–life balance is all about creating and promoting sustainable approaches to all the aspects of our life', which means that we, as truly empathetic leaders, must understand the whole gamut of emotions, life experiences, changing circumstances and inconsistencies that life throws in our faces.

Ways forward with work–life balance

As school leaders we cannot dictate what work–life balance looks like, for the very reason that it differs in definition for every stakeholder. Heads have tried to suggest that staff have an early exit on a Friday. For some this is a tremendous idea, but other teachers, particularly those in job-shares, responded with less enthusiasm. For the split class, an early finish doesn't benefit the teacher finishing on Wednesday and their colleague closing out the week will want their share of the marking completed without having to return materials on their day off.

Just as individual wellbeing agendas vary, so too will work–life balance. In the same way as providing the opportunity to manage and regulate workplace wellbeing, we need to do the same for work–life balance too. We need our teachers to thrive, socially, physically and mentally, so they are performing at their best for their pupils. Work should never overtake personal time if we are going to expect the best from our colleagues.

How to promote a healthier work–life balance

We can't dictate but we can at least guide and model what work–life balance may look like and how to lead by example. A few suggestions include:

- **Ask your teachers what they need.** Craft your wellbeing survey carefully so rather than offering an opportunity to raise negatives, what is it that they want that you can provide? Less workload? More efficient marking? PPA time at home?
- **Educate and model.** Particularly for NQTs fresh out of college who may not have had a full-time post before, the expectation they might feel to complete everything may lead to them working every hour the school is open and well into the evening. Model leaving at an earlier time at least once a week and encourage your staff to do the same.
- **Look for burnout.** Be aware of the deadlines you set and the pressure points of the school year. Spread the deadlines and give plenty of notice. In my school we have a rule that the minimum notice given for any change is one week. Support anyone clearly in need of your help and encourage your staff to look out for each other.
- **Embrace flexible working.** In a time of budget restraint the option to work part time is a financial reality as well as the opportunity for teachers to take more time for themselves.
- **Promote efficient work, not more work.** For every initiative, take some other task away. Look at marking options such as those given in Chapter 4, page 103, and reduce the need for small-scale data recording.
- **Promote healthy habits.** Encourage your staff to take time at the gym, to swim and to eat more healthily, all of which an earlier departure time may help with.
- **Prioritise tasks.** Guide staff in prioritising work and time management of key tasks.
- **Encourage breaks.** If your staff are in their rooms all day and not taking a break, this isn't healthy, workwise or socially. Look for who doesn't come to the staffroom at break or who doesn't come for lunch.

Work–life balance in the holidays

We established in Chapter 1, page 9, that wellbeing is for every day, as well as for everyone, so does every day include those days when we are not in school?

We have already discovered in Chapter 4, page 99, about the intrusion into weekends that email and planning pressures have on some teachers, but what consideration have you given to the holidays? I have noticed the concerns and worries that teachers have about the return to school each September expressed through social media and through Twitter in particular.

Each summer there are a great many teachers, particularly in the primary sector, tweeting pictures of their classrooms with the displays they have prepared, their desk layouts and nicely sharpened and organised coloured pencils. Others share images of children's books they have read in preparation for the year ahead, while secondary colleagues request support with knowledge organisers, schemes of work and other curriculum resources.

To see such enthusiasm for the profession and the year ahead will be a gratifying sight to many a headteacher, but let us balance this with some concerns. There was a lot of chatter about 'teacher dreams', even before the holiday was halfway through. Even with a rudimentary knowledge of Freudian theory, we could consider such dreams to be a sign of some underlying anxiety about the return to school. Given the impact of social media on all of us, even those supposedly hardened to 'fake news', it cannot come as any surprise that some teachers expressed a level of anxiety or guilt that they weren't as far ahead as others in their preparation for the year ahead. The more cynical users expressed a measure of dismay or dismissal of the social media posts of those spending time in school.

As school leaders we should be concerned and aware of the work–life balance of our teachers at all times, even in the long holiday. We can't be keeping in daily or weekly touch with them, because that would be intrusive. The staff WhatsApp group should ideally be muted and emails kept to a minimum and be for information only (diary dates, key reminders, class lists) and certainly not setting tasks, communicating deadlines or asking questions. Your school will be open during the holidays, for the deep clean and the maintenance jobs that cannot be done with the children around. Depending on your schedule, it may be for the whole six weeks or for as little as a fortnight. If your teachers are going in, at the very least show your face, see what they are up to and look for key signs of their level of relaxation.

On investigating the reasons why teachers were going in during their holidays in my research surveys, some common themes became apparent. The following sections will provide practical guidance for school leaders to minimise the potential impact of holiday pressures on their teaching staff.

SLT pressure

It is easy to demonise the SLT as the clipboard-wielding, target-setting and disconnected minority in a school, and while a small percentage of teachers reported that they were going in because of pressure from SLT and others said it was due to perceived pressure from other colleagues, most said they were going in through their own choice or because they hadn't completed all they needed to in the course of the summer term. Each of these scenarios has implications for the wellbeing of our teachers and all need consideration and careful handling.

While pressure from SLT was only reported by a few teachers, the manner in which this can be manifested needs a few toolkit thoughts to reduce teacher stress. Several teachers mentioned the expected arrival of Ofsted, and although we cannot predict the date of their arrival, we can be reasonably certain that the inspectors may call within a particular academic year. We have already discussed the impact of inspection on wellbeing and workload in Chapter 4, page 113, but we still need to remember that the thought of inspection does trigger anxieties among teachers and school leaders. Anything we can do to reduce stress levels will help.

Yet I have been told of schools where the definition of 'hitting the ground running' in September – or August for our friends in Scotland – means increasing levels of accountability from the start of term. If targets and progress meetings are set from the outset of term, whilst it might send the right message in terms of high standards and expectations, it also adds to the pressure on teachers who are setting out their stall with their new classes. Some teachers advised that they were spending the summer preparing new schemes of work to begin in September and others of lengthy tasks set by an incoming leadership, not in post officially until 1st September, meaning additional workload during the vacation.

Teachers have told me of receiving texts and emails from SLT asking if they were going in. Asking is different from telling, but there can be an implied meaning that 'are you' means 'you are', which very much depends on the personae our school leaders project. Should your colleagues consider that such messages imply 'letting your colleagues down' then taking a look in your empathy mirror might be advisable. Negativity flourishes where honesty and openness aren't present and what is unsaid is what is feared.

There was recently a much-shared post on Twitter of an email sent to several teachers in one department in a secondary school who had been preparing their display boards in the final week of term, not from choice but from instruction. On the last day of the term the message to the department was that some boards had missing borders and others had the wrong shade of blue. This is wrong for teacher wellbeing in a number of ways. Firstly it represents micromanagement to the nth degree; secondly it came on a round-robin email, so every recipient knew of the feedback and criticism, and unfavourable comparisons were made of another department. We would never share feedback from a lesson observation or learning walk with a third party, would we? Or tell a colleague that someone was a better teacher than them? The crux of the message though was that teachers couldn't leave for their holiday until the work was completed to expectations and the hidden message was 'this isn't good enough', which is hardly going to get the holiday off to the most auspicious start.

Keeping up with colleagues

Some teachers felt that they had to come in to prepare their classes because their colleagues were coming in. One reported to me that as they were responsible for classroom display and organisation they felt that if others were coming in, then they had to as well to set and lead an example. In one sense this can be seen as a way of bonding, team building and creating a sense of camaraderie at a less stressful time, but from another perspective this could lead to the development of a clique or perceptions of favouritism.

As a leader, your toolkit perspective needs to be focussed on this kind of observation because, though some people are able to get ahead, others may not for a plethora of reasons. For example, if you have three classes in a year group and two rooms are fully displayed and organised from the beginning of term and the other has little in place, be aware of the relationship between those three teachers. There may of course be no problems, but equally there could be the unspoken implication that they feel the other one is letting them down. Without leadership awareness, such a situation could spiral into resentment and a case of 'two against one' in terms of workload burdens, with implications for the wellbeing of everyone involved as the term unfolds. One of the most common grievances and disputes between colleagues is over perceptions of the amount and quality of work done, so don't let it fester from holiday periods.

There was also an expression of anxiety caused by looking at social media, with a number of teachers feeling anxious because of teachers around the country, and therefore not in their school, waxing lyrical about their displays, planning, books they had read and plans they had written. Of course, these aren't our colleagues, and any expectation their leaders have isn't the same as yours, but the impact of social media might be triggering 'teacher guilt' feelings. In the same manner that myths about Ofsted spread through social media, so too can such subliminal messages. However wonderful these other classrooms may look, our school expectations should not be set against those of another school in a different context hundreds of miles away.

Getting ahead

Getting prepared and getting ahead, effective use of time and being ready for the term ahead: we have all been there, or in some cases wished we had. If teachers are doing this and thinking of their wellbeing for September, then celebrate this and share their successes. At the same time, consider their wellbeing in the summer. With a recent report from the Education Support Partnership (2018) suggesting that 43 per cent of teachers were finding 'switching off' from work in the holidays increasingly difficult and that 73 per cent of teachers intended to be proactive about their wellbeing over the next summer break, the potential for burnout at an early stage of the year is all too apparent.

New schemes of work or curriculum plans, revised policies and procedures, moving between classrooms or between schools: all of these add to the pressures on our teachers. Although some leaders will dismiss this as 'part of the job', empathetic leaders will recognise the need not to overburden their colleagues, particularly at a time when relaxation needs to be the core purpose of the vacation. Many teachers have told me that they get ahead with planning and resourcing because of lack of preparation from others. Be aware that this can create a vicious circle for some teachers if they are seen as the organised ones and then their preparation is used to help those who are less efficient.

You may have teachers with high expectations and demands of themselves who don't act upon the advice to avoid work. Maybe they had some disappointing SATs results and want to be prepared for avoiding that scenario again. There are those for whom getting ahead in the holiday is a lifelong habit, perhaps ingrained from childhood – work first and have fun later. There are also those who recognise that they can reflect in the holidays, even if that reflection is in school. Some people prefer to work in school if their home environment isn't conducive to good preparation. Again we come back to the question of knowing your staff.

By all means keep the school open for periods of the holiday. Maintenance and cleaning will require this, as will examination results days. The efficient running of the school relies upon this but the message you convey in your days and times of holiday opening can speak volumes.

Do you know who is going in and how often? Do you know if they are making effective use of their time? Who is there to see this: heads and deputies or the office and cleaning staff? If your teachers are getting things ready in the last week of July or in early August, is this because they simply want to be ready or is it that they anticipate your demands in September? This may say more about you than about them and also indicate the culture that you have developed in your school.

Catching up

Alongside the teachers wishing to be ahead of the game, we have many teachers who will go into school in the first days of their holiday because there are tasks they haven't finished. If these are jobs that need the children out of the way, such as backing new boards, labelling books or even emptying the cupboards then that is a fair use of time.

If teachers are using the holiday to catch up on tasks they were not able to complete in the summer term, however, take a long, hard look at your timetabling and your annual diary. A number of teachers reported doing assessments in the last week with a data drop in the first week of term. From a primary or a secondary perspective, this makes little sense as pupils are not going to work at their best at that time of year when the end-of-term assemblies and school trips are greater priorities, and if teachers are leaving, is their focus going to be upon the accuracy of their data?

The second half of the summer term has become increasingly stressful in recent years. The stereotype of Year 6 giving their afternoons to games of rounders has been challenged by the revised writing frameworks and moderation process taking the assessment focus well into June in English schools. For secondary teachers their 'gained time' with the departure of Year 11 soon evaporates with preparations for the transition of Year 7. Increasingly detailed transition forms, some several pages long, add to the workload of both camps. Add to the mix the administration that needs to be completed, useful or otherwise as Chapter 4, page 99, details, and increasingly short tempers in our now regular heatwaves, it is little wonder that some tasks will remain incomplete.

This is why workload needs to be addressed and unnecessary tasks eliminated. Teachers feeling stressed from work that is incomplete, particularly if left by staff leaving, need to be supported and recognised. There is a huge difference here between the department using the 'wrong' backing paper and teachers with burdensome tasks to complete.

Allowing sufficient time at the beginning of the new term to prepare is not always possible. One or two full-on training days followed by the arrival of the pupils the next day allows no time unless your teachers have spent some of the summer in school. Some schools allow for preparation time on those days; others do not. Last-minute demands and short-notice changes immediately add pressure. If you have teachers staying until 6pm the day before the children arrive, these could be your candidates for early burnout.

Why do we get stressed in the holiday?

Many non-teachers look with envy at the six-week break in the summer, without realising that for most of us it takes a good fortnight to unwind from school mode. It takes some time to relax completely, if indeed that is possible. The Education Support Partnership (2018) research suggested that financial and health concerns were a cause of anxiety for some teachers in the holiday period. Significantly, and related to the workplace, a number raised the matter of GCSE and A-level results and concern over the performance of their pupils, a number mentioned job security and a similar number noted the professional relationships with their colleagues.

While your wellbeing toolkit can't do much for examination results, it can make us aware of some of these other concerns, particularly relating to positive school cultures. Relationships with colleagues were mentioned to me by several teachers, some reporting a lack of trust among their team as a reason for getting stressed in the holiday. Others mentioned 'tricky' colleagues who might be short tempered or less than polite in their language.

Some others were clear: 'They don't and they won't [support wellbeing],' one very direct reply said, alongside others who reported that wellbeing wasn't a priority during the school year so certainly wasn't during the holiday. Deadlines set for the first week in September are a clear indicator of wellbeing being low on the agenda. If teachers have had a tough time during the year, six long weeks to think further about this, particularly away from any support, is naturally going to make them wary. Unresolved issues from the previous year, behaviour management, parental relationships, grievances and potential capability procedures may leave the confidence of some staff hanging by a thread.

The way that the term ends can also leave a sour taste for some. Where the language of leadership is harsh and critical, particularly in primary school where SATs results arrive with a week of term to go, teachers can feel demoralised. Interim leadership, often charged with turning around a school quickly, may also be overly negative, especially if there is no investment in wellbeing in a short-term position. Doubts about the dynamics of the team they are returning to can weigh heavily on the mind over a long break. Nothing worries a teacher like a set of shifting goalposts.

It is equally true that, though there are some expectations of what would be done in a six-week break, our colleagues' summers will all look very different. For all those who might be away for a month or more, others will take weekends or take no break at all as money is tight. Some of us are partnered by another teacher, but for those with a partner in commerce or another aspect of public service, there is the potential of up to six weeks home alone. Colleagues with young children will clearly make them their priority. For some teachers the thought of returning in September and facing the small talk about the holiday fills them with dread. We can't avoid the post-holiday chatter, but leaders need to be aware of how this affects our staff.

Think too of our new teachers. Research from Leeds Beckett University (2018) suggests high levels of stress and anxiety among trainee teachers and up to one fifth reporting their ITT course had caused symptoms of depression. Almost half of the sample felt a lack of confidence. Though the sample researched was small, we should be concerned that so many of our youngest teachers say they cannot achieve a good work–life balance or maintain good social relationships. With such large numbers of teachers dropping out of the profession in the first few years, we need to be thinking of how our school culture supports those new teachers arriving fresh each September so that their wellbeing is supported from the outset of their career, to build the resilience that will sustain them as they build their experience.

Good SLT practice

Let us think positively though. Many teachers reported that their SLT positively modelled wellbeing strategies for the holidays. The most encouraging were those who set deadlines for the end of term, meaning that pressure of target setting, policy writing and new initiatives did not drag into the break or the next term. One school even organised a shutdown of their network server in the first week of the holiday to encourage non-engagement with school activities.

The below are some key action points for school leaders to ensure wellbeing remains a priority even in the school holidays:

- Actively model wellbeing strategies to encourage unwinding and recharging.
- Address all priorities before the end of term and have no surprises or new initiatives on returning in September.

- Be transparent about not answering emails. Actively encourage the 'out of office' automated answer.
- Drop any expectation for analysis of pupil progress.
- Only send work emails in the last week of the holiday and consider a team-building day before the end of the break.
- Timetables, key dates, duties and rotas should all be distributed before term ends.

- Make it very clear that perfect classrooms are not the expectation for the first day back and recognise that it does take time. A 'warm' or 'soft' start to the term sends a strong message about school culture; don't forget the deadlines though because you can be too soft.
- Be in school, particularly for new teachers, to support and help locate resources.

These are the simplest things to organise and to say. Authentic leaders telling staff not to come in mean it; where the interpretation of 'don't come in' is that there is an unspoken expectation to do so, have a think about the culture you project.

Our holiday periods should not be absorbed by worry or concern but should be a time of relaxation, celebration and reflection. Does your culture support this model?

Case study: Wellbeing is for everyone

Lessness Heath Primary School

Lessness Heath Primary School nestles hidden behind the 1930s houses of a busy road in Belvedere in the London Borough of Bexley. A large school with three forms of entry and over 630 children, Lessness Heath serves an increasingly diverse community with families from the whole range of socio-economic backgrounds with a catchment covering the privately owned houses nearby and the estate further down the hill. Though with a free school meals figure of 18 per cent, considerably less than that at Parklands (see page 69), many of the issues remain the same.

Lessness Heath came to my attention when the school was the first in the UK to be awarded the Wellbeing Award for Schools, created by Optimus Education and the National Children's Bureau. Much attention in the national and local press followed, including an appearance on BBC London News with a specific focus on the 'Family Matters' programme the school runs, which is attended by some 150 parents.

Kelly Hannaghan leads the programme of wellbeing at Lessness Heath. Though not a teacher, Kelly is from an education background and crucially has the support and backing of the headteacher, Katy O'Connor. Wellbeing at this school is not passed along as described in Chapter 1, page 11; it is in the hands of someone who believes in a clear vision of wellbeing, and this is bought into by the headteacher and the rest of SLT. Kelly initially came to the school as a wellbeing consultant, having established her own business, but is now employed full time by the school.

When Kelly first visited the school, she found a staff with low morale. The school had previously been rated 'inadequate' by Ofsted and placed into special measures. The school was under pressure and monitoring visits hadn't gone well. Complaints were made regularly by parents; there were inconsistencies and gaps in monitoring systems; problems slipped through the net; and there was a lack of visible consistency from school leaders. Teachers were anxious to talk to parents about behaviour and learning, children lacked resilience and provision for their emotional health was lacking. As Katy told me, 'Nobody seemed to like each other.'

Subsequently taken into a MAT, The Primary First Trust, the school has been on a remarkable journey, attaining both the Wellbeing Award and a 'Good with outstanding features' inspection judgement in December 2017.

I visited Lessness Heath in July 2018, at the business end of a long, hot summer, to find what the secret to their success was. Unaware of the material I had written so far, both Kelly and Katy used the language and expressed the values that *The Wellbeing Toolkit* lives by. Katy told me that, as the headteacher, the most important elements for her were relationships and culture within the school. Where these were invisible or lacking beforehand, they are abundantly apparent now. 'Look after your staff and they will look after you,' Katy announced, summarising the philosophy that underpins the work at the school. Unbeknown to her these were exactly the same words used by Chris Dyson at Parklands and that I have used in my professional development presentations. The language of those leaders who understand wellbeing is universal.

Wellbeing is a whole-school focus; it is lived, breathed and built into the language of the school community. It is in the culture of the school because everyone knows it counts. Wellbeing truly is for every day at Lessness Heath; it is for everyone: children, parents, staff and the community. The award is the icing on the cake.

Kelly is very passionate about wellbeing and understands that there is no one-size-fits-all model for it. It took some time to win over some members of staff, which was quite natural where trust and collaboration had been eroded beforehand and also reflected a fear of change, which is another instinctive human response. Her starting point is language; observing Kelly with children, SLT, teachers and other staff the tone is consistent, positive and reflective. 'What can we do to improve your wellbeing?' was and still is a frequently asked question.

The language of positivity has drip fed into the attitudes of the children too. They have felt empowered through initiatives to build their resilience. There is provision to support the children's mental health, supported by organisations such as the Anna Freud Centre and Young Minds. Play therapy, draw and talk, and 'chill out club' all support children with their emotional needs. Parents are supported through the school's own 'Family Matters' workshops supporting family health and wellbeing, positive relationships, healing trauma and positive parenting strategies.

The staffroom has a staff wellbeing board, including 'Shout Outs' acknowledging the contributions made by colleagues, a list of regular nights out for team building and a range of other wellbeing initiatives, including massage for those who want it. This echoes the wellbeing displays in each classroom.

Wellbeing is, however, more than just on display at Lessness Heath. It is embedded in the culture of the school. Concerns in the wellbeing survey are written into the action plan. Support at stressful times is provided sensitively and with a flexible approach. All staff receive training in managing stressful incidents. Verbal, written and electronic communication ensures staff are well informed in advance and in detail about events and concerns. Staff absent, either signed off unwell or on parental leave, are kept in regular contact and support is provided upon their return. The wellbeing philosophy is shared by the after-school club too; though a tenant of the school, the principles and practices extend to this provider and their staff too.

The ethos and the culture of the school are positive and everyone is valued. These are not mere empty statements on a policy document; they are embedded in the relationships between the staff, children and parents to enable and secure an effective environment for teaching and learning, for living and growing. Kelly and Katy know what makes the teachers and other staff tick. They know that for some people wellbeing is served with a grumble or two in the staffroom but others will find other outlets. The members of SLT and teaching staff I met told me that they felt empowered to look after their wellbeing and comfortable to raise any concerns that they had. Two teaching assistants told me that their wellbeing is served by walking Lola the therapy dog. Lola is another important part of the school wellbeing jigsaw. She has her own blog too. A dog with a blog: how cool is that?

Kelly is a bundle of energy, dedicated to the wellbeing of the whole school community. Her philosophy, which Katy fully supports, enables the whole staff to speak honestly and openly about their wellbeing experience. The 'sideways-in' model of wellbeing is unmistakably in operation here, supported by SLT but driven by everyone.

Lessness Heath is, in short, a happy place to be.

The contrast between Parklands (see page 69) and Lessness Heath is marked in the styles of their leaders. Whereas Chris is a big personality, Kelly and Katy are quieter in their approach. In both schools though, wellbeing for staff, children and the wider community is at the heart of everything that they do. In both schools the values of *The Wellbeing Toolkit* are there for all to see: collaboration, respect, trust, support, resilience and courage, empathy by the bucketload, a hearty respect for the valuable time of all colleagues and most definitely a sense of celebration. These schools didn't need this book to tell them that.

Toolkit takeaways

Work–life balance

The definitions here can only give a taster of what work–life balance may look like for your staff. If you are following the toolkit principles, then the essential element is knowing your staff. We aren't going to guess what work–life balance looks like, so why not ask?

In my findings, several teachers had been told that work–life balance wasn't a priority, some had been told that it wasn't achievable and others had been bluntly told, 'It will never happen here' by other teachers and in some cases by the headteacher. A failure to fully acknowledge the place and importance of work–life balance will send the message that staff happiness is of low or no priority.

Holidays

To protect the wellbeing of your staff during their vital downtime over the holidays, think about doing the following:

- Tell your colleagues to set up the 'out of office' function on their email.
- Keep any emails to information only: timetables, diaries and rotas. Ideally, send these round before term ends.
- Never ask for anything during the holidays. Be organised and have it done beforehand.
- Mute the staff WhatsApp group.
- Be very aware of the stress on teachers at the end of term and don't let them leave feeling anxious.
- If your other senior leaders are ramping up the pressure on less experienced staff, rein them in.
- Be aware of the unspoken pressure that some teachers feel because others seem 'more organised'.
- Be aware of who is keeping up and who is catching up.

7 Births, marriages and deaths

Chapter overview

In this chapter we will discuss how the principles in the wellbeing toolkit can be applied in supporting staff through pregnancy and parental leave, through relationship breakdown and through bereavement. We will cover:

- **Fair and principled approaches to a range of issues relating to pregnancy, IVF and parenthood.**
- **Sensitive approaches to relationship breakdown.**
- **Supporting individuals and the school community at a time of loss.**

The next part will consider some of the real-life scenarios where the use of *The Wellbeing Toolkit* will be put to the test. Workload and day-to-day interactions are only part of wellbeing, as we have established, but when life intervenes there is another level of challenge to consider.

Here we will consider the implications for staff wellbeing of pregnancy and parenthood and how as leaders our mindset needs to change to reflect the personal circumstances of our teachers. We will further explore wellbeing to support those whose relationship is under strain, before turning our thoughts to supporting colleagues who suffer bereavement. The last part of the chapter focusses on the challenge that the misuse of social media platforms can potentially present to the wellbeing and welfare of all our colleagues.

From here to maternity: wellbeing through pregnancy and beyond

The news of a pregnancy on the staff is a cause of great happiness and celebration, and headteachers will be delighted that the personal happiness of their staff will soon result in a new arrival. There will be many a headteacher, however, who will tell you that their heart sinks at the news of a pregnancy among the staff. For some headteachers, this means losing a talented teacher on maternity leave for an uncertain period of time; for others, the first thought is going to be appointments in school time, morning sickness, risk assessments, requests for flexible working and time taken for a child being ill. Headteachers also need to consider that couples can share parental leave and that also those teachers adopting are entitled to adoption leave too (visit this link for more information: https://www.gov.uk/shared-parental-leave-and-pay). Your thoughts, words and actions will say much about you and your attitude towards wellbeing so far as it relates to parenthood.

For those who fall into the second category of school leaders (those worrying about practical matters), this doesn't necessarily make you hard and uncaring. These are important considerations with budgetary implications and challenges for the management of a school. Though a school cannot necessarily plan for teachers expecting a family, it can at the very least be anticipated. In a profession where 75 per cent of teachers are women – 83 per cent in primary (Department for Education, 2017b) – it is not beyond reasonable expectation that some, if not all, of your recently married or partnered staff will fall pregnant. I recently visited a three-form-entry primary school, where there were seven teachers, all of whom married over one summer, who were on or about to begin their second maternity leave. The school business manager had built this into their section of the school development plan as a result.

Babies are one of life's pleasing consequences, though not for everyone of course. In the spirit of *The Wellbeing Toolkit* values, our first response should be one of celebration. Bringing a child into the world is the most significant event in a person's life and if the journey to conception has been littered by frustrations and obstacles, the relief and joy will be immeasurable. It would take a cold and detached person, even one with no interest in becoming a parent, not to share the delight at the news of an imminent arrival.

Babies change lives and lifestyles too. The teacher who used to be in at seven o'clock each morning might now be regularly arriving at half past eight instead because they now have a childminder, nursery or loving grandparent to consider. The other end of the day will also change for similar reasons. This does not make them any less of a teacher. Becoming a parent doesn't turn the brain to mush!

Wellbeing and parenthood go hand in hand. In my research, my general questioning revealed a number of concerns about parenthood and a more specific survey included areas to share more widely. This section will discuss some of the wellbeing implications for schools.

Poor treatment

While there are many schools where there is absolutely fair and sensitive care for expectant and returning mothers, there are many incidences of unfair treatment by schools and in some cases of poor attitudes from staff other than school leaders.

A number of teachers reported in my survey that they felt concerned about telling their headteacher about a pregnancy. In some cases other staff intervened to warn the head to react appropriately. If there is this aspect of fear, then a look at the atmosphere conveyed needs to be taken and acted upon. Comments such as 'nobody else can get pregnant this year' might be a throwaway line or a lame attempt at humour, but also a very insensitive intrusion into the most personal of life decisions. It might be a tricky time in school, with potential restructure, Ofsted pending or maybe an investigation of some kind, but biology cannot be put on hold. Sly and oblique comments relating to the 'inconvenience' that anticipated maternity or paternity leave would cause are just unfair, especially to someone who may be feeling emotionally and physically vulnerable. The school will move on regardless of who is there or not, and this includes the headteacher.

Headteachers taking maternity or paternity leave are not exempt from stressful experiences either. Several have felt under pressure from governors to guarantee exactly how long they would be absent from school and what arrangements would be in place to cover their time away. While an outline plan could be given, nothing is certain with pregnancy and childbirth so a little more humanity might be expected here.

Of more concern were those women who said that their maternity marked the beginning of a campaign to drive them from the school. Being told not to bother applying for a promotion, one that may even have been targeted for that teacher before their change of circumstance, smacks immediately of discrimination.

Asking for the resignation of a colleague returning for the last period after maternity or paternity leave has finished, though they had indicated that they would be going, is bordering what isn't acceptable. To ask the office staff to make the call lacks any compassion or moral responsibility too.

Keeping in touch and returning to work

The school here needs to find a happy medium between keeping someone in the loop and communication overload. By all means keep someone on the weekly business 'all staff' email and any staff WhatsApp groups. After all, they have the option to leave or mute the latter.

Many respondents to my surveys felt that the communication they had during their maternity or paternity leave was excellent. They were made extremely welcome on their keeping in touch (KIT) days and, on their full return, a buddy was often in place to deliver gifts from staff and parents and to help them keep up with the professional and personal chatter that might have been missed. KIT days with planning and a feeling of purpose can help ease someone back after a period away. Easing someone back with a gentle transition period and an acceptance of a flexible or part-time working pattern shows a suitable level of compassion and principled leadership.

Unhappy experiences of KIT often left teachers feeling isolated. Leaving teachers to chase enquiries for themselves or to negotiate a change of terms over the phone rather than face-to-face says much of the lack of support in some establishments. A lack of a suitable space for a new mother to express milk, insensitive treatment such as others discussing a return to work with the knowledge but without the presence of the teacher concerned, and requests to finish certain work projects during maternity leave are all examples of treatment with no empathy and little sensitivity to the change in personal circumstances.

A number of new parents felt that they had been pushed out during their leave. Subsequent time in their school was short after their return, which is brutal in a place they loved and embraced beforehand. Others felt that colleagues had got their feet under the table during their absence and some felt their authority and reputation had been undermined at the same time. Others were given not class responsibility as they had requested but tasks such as PPA cover with the pressures of planning for unfamiliar classes, subjects and behaviour management strategies.

IVF

For those who have had difficulties in conception, IVF is often their last hope. It is, however, not a simple process and can be an emotional rollercoaster to experience, especially given that pregnancy rates for treatment are less than 50 per cent (SART, 2018). Empathy for colleagues in this situation needs to be absolute and unquestioned. If staff choose not to disclose that they are undergoing treatment, that is their decision and it needs to be respected. Unless able to afford private treatment, colleagues will need appointments in school time, which will mean indicating to the headteacher why such absences are needed. Their confidentiality must be respected. Inevitably there is going to be gossip and possibly some resentment about why somebody is having regular time off and it is imperative that this is shut down and also that timetables of other staff aren't impacted. IVF isn't a short-term process; couples may go through up to five years of treatment. Support your colleague through this and your empathy and compassion will be recognised.

Have a heart

Please recognise that there is no such thing as a 'routine pregnancy' and be prepared for this. Morning sickness is unpleasant, disorienting and not confined to the morning. The recent experience of the Duchess of Cambridge has highlighted just how debilitating the condition can be for some women. Kate didn't require a 'supply royal' to cover her duties, but school realities need leaders to anticipate such eventualities. A two- to three-week period of sickness might need some cover and juggling of the timetable – it is a condition, not an illness, and it will pass. No expectant mother should be made to feel guilty.

As I've mentioned, there are many couples for whom conceiving a child is difficult or impossible. For people in this situation, to see colleague after colleague celebrating an imminent arrival can be heartbreaking, particularly if following unsuccessful cycles of treatment. To have a colleague or their partner miscarry is equally upsetting. Those feeling most self-critical may feel like they have failed in some way. Though there is a greater openness and less stigma about the discussion of mental health issues, this is one area where your colleague might close up and not talk about their feelings because of the sensitivity involved.

Please remember that a new child isn't an easy life transition. When one or more has difficulty settling into a sleeping pattern, when childminders let parents down or if settling into a routine at nursery is difficult, these things all require a hearty dose of compassion and some short-term planning for flexibility to allow support for changes. Is it too much to ask for the headteacher to cover the last lesson once in a while for example?

This is a key point for the empathy tool to be employed, with a healthy dose of compassion. Having an open-door policy is very different from an open-heart policy. This doesn't mean being a 'soft touch' and is not an instant fix, but sending a clear message through values and actions that you can be trusted and that confidentiality is absolutely guaranteed will give colleagues the confidence to share just what they are going through. Knowing that you give the time just to listen, understand, and be there with a box of tissues and a hug if necessary is all that they need.

Don't forget the other parent

In looking after parental wellbeing, the role of the other parent can often be overlooked. The change in lifestyle affects not only the mother who is giving birth to the baby, but the father or other partner too. When I became a parent, paternity leave was a mere two days and with a sense of mistiming that babies naturally employ, the arrival of my daughters during the nativity season and then in SATs week had an impact on timetabling. These days there is a greater consideration for new fathers but male teachers have told me that some of them have faced criticism in school for taking their full entitlement. Some of this has come from school leaders but many have had sharp words from other colleagues.

Nobody should be judged for using what is rightly and contractually their time to take. There would never be a criticism levelled at a person signed off unwell for a fortnight taking that time off, so equally there should be none here too. Indications were that there was some form of resentment at someone taking this time, often from those without children or without an awareness of how life changes.

A new baby requires life adjustments for both parents and the first nappy change, middle-of-the-night feed or episode of projectile vomiting is often enough to make you wonder what you have let yourself in for. As soon as your child is ill for the first time the concern is natural and fearful. Try having to face that with no paternity leave left as I did when my eldest daughter was hospitalised at only three days old.

New parents can feel vulnerable too and leaders need to look for this and intervene if necessary. The new father told that he was using his new baby 'as an excuse' faced an inexcusable intrusion into his lifestyle by a line manager clearly immune to the emotions of parenthood. This is only going to add to the vulnerability that some colleagues may be feeling.

It should not be forgotten that a colleague's partner may have developed post-natal depression, something they may not wish to share. New fathers too can suffer from a form of post-natal depression as they come to terms with the changes in their life. Sleep deprivation is physically and mentally exhausting and a perceived lack of interest and social withdrawal may follow. Keep an eye out for your colleagues and an ear open for unsympathetic comments.

Growing up

Babies obviously don't stay that way forever. As they grow, demands change and lifestyle patterns and behaviours alter; this is a natural consequence of being a parent. They start school, they get sick, they have siblings, and they cause their parents problems, even the 'perfect' ones!

The Wellbeing Toolkit doesn't need to be tucked away once the school babies are out of nappies. It needs to be very much in mind, because those lifestyle changes mentioned earlier include the significant events in a child's life where the presence of parents means so much; if you get grumpy because the Mary or the camel has waved at their mum at the most hallowed moment of the nativity, just remember for the child and parents this precious moment of eye contact is a moment of affirmation and pride.

Yet in my research there were many teachers who said that they couldn't attend their child's nativity, leaving assembly or performance. Reasons given included 'inconvenience' or 'their mother/grandparents will be there'; this is absolutely one of the coldest and most inhuman things I have heard. I know that there will be some who will say a five-year-old's nativity is nothing to do with wellbeing, but this would ignore the message of this book: wellbeing is holistic, for every day, for everyone and it is for life, including life's significant moments.

Children will also fall ill. Some of our teachers might be able to call upon their own parents or family network, but many will have relocated or lost their parents. It is unlikely that a childminder would look after a child with chicken pox and anyway the child would want to be with their parents when unwell. Children can fall seriously ill with life-threatening or potentially life-changing conditions. Several teachers have told me that they have had 'Can't your wife look after him?' as a response. Again this shows a complete lack of empathy with the emotions and fears of parents and also a rather sexist assumption that the wife isn't in a significant job role too. In my experience, teachers and other staff who are given time when their child is unwell will repay that time, not so they don't miss out on a wage, but to repay the care, trust and loyalty shown to them in the first place.

Children will have their problems too. School is unlikely to pass incident free and teachers' children are just as likely to get into scrapes as everyone else. They will also have exam stresses, relationship issues, school journeys and open days. They will move schools at 11 and need to spend time looking at potential choices. Each circumstance, and similar, with a considered and empathetic approach can be supported and, as a principle, be built into a good wellbeing policy.

Marriages and relationships

We all love a teacher wedding. The anticipation of it, the positive atmosphere generated and the sense of celebration at the forthcoming union of one of our colleagues represent an opportunity for the whole staff to mark the occasion. This is a significant event in a colleague's life as they embark upon a happy and healthy relationship.

A sad reality though is that teacher relationships do break up. Sadder still is that some break down because of the pressures of school life, of school pushing out other priorities, of workload eating into the weekends and evenings more than it should. Relationships also obviously break down for a range of other reasons unrelated to work. The role of heads here is to be empathetic, understanding and non-judgemental.

Should a teacher express concerns about their workload impacting on their relationships, please take it seriously. We can all, regardless of our length of service, identify at least one marriage that has fractured partly because school gets in the way. It is the right, indeed the need, of all our colleagues to have a romantic relationship of their choosing and to have a social life. As we saw earlier, schools with intrusive planning requirements are going to interfere with the social lives of their teachers. If your teachers are losing a relationship because of school and workload, the school is likely to lose them in return.

Another acid test of our empathy is in the support we give to a colleague who is going through a rocky patch, experiencing a marital breakdown or dealing with the consequences of separation or divorce. Again, confidentiality has to be watertight as a colleague is unlikely in the early days to want to share this information with the whole staff. Rumour and gossip also need to be managed and quashed to protect your colleague from questioning from staff and especially parents. Nobody need know the details or causes of the split and, as we saw on page 81, we don't want to see this on social media either.

The most important way to support though is simply being there for your colleague. They might be in an uncomfortable position with their, or their partner's, family. There might be a feeling of embarrassment, especially where a marriage or partnership breaks down after a short period of time. Being the 'rock' or the shoulder to cry on, the non-judgemental but totally reliable source of support, will demonstrate your strength as a leader of wellbeing.

Managing bereavement

One unquestionable test of the school leader's authentic ability to lead wellbeing in a values-led manner comes with one of life's sad but inevitable outcomes. Whether you are faced with dealing with the passing of a colleague's parents, in-laws or other family member, or the more daunting loss of a colleague, or worse still a pupil, a principles-based approach sets us in good stead for managing the scenario. Crucially, decisions reached here will be spur-of-the-moment ones; if you live your values, your tough choices will be the right ones, as trust, compassion, empathy and respect direct your actions.

Yet I heard while researching this book of some examples of leaders lacking in empathy for members of their staff suffering through a period of terminal illness, mourning and grief. Remember, bereavement affects not only your colleague, but their partner or spouse, children and dependants, and other members of their family. This is a stark reminder that wellbeing leadership, good or otherwise, reaches beyond the confines of the school.

Losing a family member

Losing a member of your family is tough. However hard-faced and unemotional someone might appear in public, behind that mask is the full range of human emotions. Some people are good at holding it all in, traditional stiff-upper-lip style. Others will struggle to hold back the tears. If you genuinely know your colleagues, you can tell who will keep things private and who will be more open about their feelings, but in both cases your support will be appreciated. Offering support alone, the 'I'm here if you need to talk' approach, isn't enough, as that puts the onus on the other party. Proactive leaders will anticipate this. Asking a colleague in just to talk is an effective means of support. Don't rampage straight in with 'How are you coping after the death of...', as this shows little sensitivity. Try not raising the matter at all. If it comes up in conversation, so be it. The simple act of talking, taking the time to be there, may be enough to show your empathy.

There are three stages to consider: the period of illness leading up to the loss, the time between the passing and the funeral, and the time of mourning. The first and last could be of indeterminate time and herein lies the test of empathy and compassion over cold organisation.

When a colleague comes to you with the news of a terminal illness in the family, is your reaction one of shock at the news or one of how your school is going to be affected by potential staff absence? Of course both need to be considered, but when a response to the second is blurted out involuntarily or otherwise, empathy doesn't look high on the agenda. One example would be in the case of an in-law falling ill; the response, 'Well, can't your wife/husband/partner be responsible for the hospital visits?', with some variation, has been mentioned to me. This shows no empathy for the family dynamic, for cultural considerations and for the impact on the mental wellbeing of other family members. However well you know your team, you are not going to know about family closeness or tensions, nor how the pressures of a terminal illness are going to affect your colleague.

It is at this time that empathy and compassion need to be unpacked from your toolkit, together with a healthy portion of confidentiality. Some people will share the sad news with their colleagues, because this is the comfort blanket they may need, but equally others may want this kept quiet. Allowing for hospital visits in work time is inevitably going to result in some gossip and some more direct questioning about an absence. Be aware of this and kill the gossip. If you have a strong culture of confidentiality this is easier, but you may have to have a few stiff conversations to shore up the privacy that some circumstances demand. Have some key people onside because there are going to be timetable changes and cover issues. Being flexible in planning and being fair to everyone else may need some unexpected arrangements; it is the inflexible leader who allows such tragic circumstances to add unnecessarily to workload.

In the case of a lengthy illness, the final days may be spent in hospital or in a hospice and this is the time to cut your colleague some slack. They may be repaying your support by a full day at work, but if they need to go at half past three each afternoon, let them go. The staff meeting, the display board, the marking they have missed can wait. If your empathy cascades down to your team, others will step in and support with the essential tasks.

When the time comes, despite some people saying they will be all right, they aren't going to be all right. An empathetic leader will give time off before and maybe after the funeral. In the majority of cases a colleague who loses a family member will have said goodbye to a parent, grandparent or in-law. In the case of parents, there may be no end of legal and probate matters to attend to. Many teachers will live some distance from their home town (or country) and may need to be away for some time. Insisting on a return to work isn't going to help anyone. Whether it is a week or two that you allow, think of people, not pounds. Your trust and loyalty will be repaid by staff who are looked after.

This brings us to funeral attendance. I have been told of some schools that only permit staff to attend the funerals of immediate relatives and allow only unpaid attendance for other occasions. Where does this leave us with colleagues who want to attend the funeral of family friends? I have also heard of the refusal of leave 'because it would inconvenience others', which lacks any empathy whatsoever. Many colleagues are happy to make their own cover arrangements, swapping PPA time or making up time elsewhere, so as not to cause any disruption to the time of others – no 'inconvenience' here. Being able to attend a funeral allows for 'closure' for some people and for others it is an expectation of their culture. Not being able to say a proper farewell can trigger feelings of guilt. A flexible and thoughtful approach to funeral attendance is therefore an important wellbeing consideration.

The final stage to consider is probably the most difficult and challenging: the grieving process and recovery. Grief is draining, physically and emotionally, and anyone who has lost a parent or in-law may run on nervous energy for a few weeks and outwardly appear to be holding it all together, but as with any mental health issue the scars are hidden. Keeping an eye on them in an unobtrusive way is a key strategy. Rather than a school leader taking the prime responsibility, there may be a trusted friend who is better positioned to help and listen; a teacher who began at the same time as a colleague or maybe someone who has been through the same experience themselves of late.

To leave someone to come back without support shows a lack of empathy, though a number of teachers have told me that they had support before their bereavement but little afterwards. One said:

> *'It was a case of "it's over now, you can get back to work" and "just get over it" from some staff and little more than lip service from the head who told me I had taken enough time off.'*

Space and time to talk would have been more beneficial. Counselling services or providing the number of the Education Support Partnership are the very least that can be offered. Thinking about key dates, such as the anniversary of the passing or birthdays, and how your colleague is going to face the next long holiday (given that school might be a refuge from the pain) needs to be in the forefront of our wellbeing planning too. Empathetic school leaders will set themselves a written or digital reminder of these significant times and will act upon it. Though it might not seem much, never underestimate the positive impact of a simple yet considered note in a card or a text message to express your sincerest thoughts.

Losing a colleague

Many of us will have been through the scenario of losing a colleague. If suffering from a terminal illness, there will be the obvious sadness but also a sense of preparedness if the passing was expected. Please respect the wishes of your colleague and their family, but also prepare your staff. Let them know and tell them face-to-face, however hard this might seem, because electronic communication of such news would lack all empathy.

In the case of the sudden and unexpected death of a colleague, thinking on one's feet and managing human responses tests our leadership resolve.

This is exactly the situation faced in my experience. We lost one of our teaching assistants suddenly and unexpectedly. Without going into details, how we managed at this sad time echoed our school values. Instinct kicks in; though we had a bereavement policy, we made decisions driven by wellbeing and empathy, not by paperwork. Communication needs to be sensitive; we told everyone face-to-face, except those part-time colleagues who weren't working that day who had a phone call, because we didn't want anyone to hear from parents or social media first. Parents were written to, the letters in sealed envelopes so children didn't hear before they did. The parents of the classes affected were told first and given the option of discussing the passing with their children or leaving it to us.

Having support and distinct levels of qualification available is important, particularly when telling the children. Children react differently to such news. Some knew already, but of those who didn't there was a mixture of instant or delayed emotional reaction, but also of confusion and anger: the latter impacted children who had recently lost older family members. Having a trained counsellor present gave the children a chance to talk freely, and having the SENDCo there too helped the autistic pupils who had different understandings of what death was.

Think of the staff who provide this support too, because grief is exhausting, the emotion is draining and the intensity in a short time frame – two days in this case – overwhelming. It takes some timetable shuffling and flexibility, and a commitment to our wellbeing values, but think of the impact of such events on your colleagues; give them time to come to terms with events, space to express themselves and the chance for some relief from their duties for some recovery time.

Losing a pupil

I have had colleagues and friends who have had to face the death of a child in their school. It is a traumatic experience, especially so if sudden and unexpected. Arguably this is going to have a greater impact than the loss of an adult because the community affected will have different bonds; this is a friend, a sibling, a daughter or son, a grandchild.

The same wellbeing tools need to be unpacked: empathy and compassion in particular. This needs though to be backed with expert help. Some of the best resources to access are provided by Child Bereavement UK. Their website provides a wealth of expertly informed and practical strategies that acknowledge the time-critical conditions that such sad circumstances bring. The best advice for the loss of a child is: be open, be empathetic but seek expert advice.

Toolkit takeaways

With each of the scenarios explored in this chapter, the element of *The Wellbeing Toolkit* to employ here is common sense, alongside sensitivity and consistency. Though birth, relationship breakdown and bereavement are part of life, they aren't part of a school development plan.

Though we can anticipate our teachers planning to start a family and can plan for a period of leave, we can't think ahead to life's crisis points. If we have a principled approach to our wellbeing, the response will be measured, rather than panicked.

Conclusion

Why does wellbeing in our schools and for all of our staff matter? I hope *The Wellbeing Toolkit* has made you realise why. Ultimately, wellbeing matters because it is about relationships, and it is about your team. I have made a number of references to sports psychology in the text. There is one more that, even if you have no interest in sport, I feel you would embrace.

The England football team went beyond all expectations at the 2018 World Cup in Russia. Before the game against Sweden, the BBC broadcast an extract from a documentary about the life of Sir Bobby Robson, in which his widow, Lady Elsie, read a handwritten list of how the former England manager sought to motivate his players. The list is relevant to promoting a team spirit in any environment. It is just as relevant to promoting an effective wellbeing agenda and relates to the values detailed throughout this book. With respect to the memory of Sir Bobby, I have included his advice below, with my addendums in italics, though most of his points need no clarification:

'To build a team of motivated players a good coach *(school leader)* should:

1. Be able to control himself before he can control them (the team – *the teachers*).
2. Be passionate about the subject (in this case football – but it could be anything, e.g. cars, electrical goods, furniture, *education*!).
3. Be open-minded – a good listener.
4. [Be] a winner: single-minded about the ultimate outcome. *(There are no winners in our game, but we can be single-minded in attaining our goals.)*
5. [Be] honest – to gain respect – fair.
6. Command discipline.
7. Set good examples.
8. Understand individuals (what makes them tick).
9. React positively to criticism. Decrease the stress.
10. Be positive and confident to give confidence to others.
11. Be trustworthy.' (Bobby Robson in Fawbert, 2018)

Wise words indeed.

Scan education feeds on Twitter or Facebook over the course of a week or so and the debates and discussion will cover topics as diverse as phonics, behaviour and exclusions, curriculum and class organisation. Wellbeing is often discussed, most often in a positive manner. There is recognition, I believe, in teacher social media, that wellbeing is an area of concern and one ripe for development and innovation in our schools.

The Wellbeing Toolkit will hopefully go some way to unlocking minds and opening eyes to the depth of the issues in regard to the mental and physical wellbeing of our school staff and to challenging the barriers to it. The culture in our schools is the key determinant of how wellbeing can be led and managed. Sort the culture and we allow wellbeing to thrive; leave it to fester and it becomes toxic and challenging and permits the growth of bullying with all the implications this brings for retention and recruitment.

Wellbeing in our schools is also down to individual choice. Work–life balance has no clear definition as it differs for everyone. For every teacher who stays prepping and planning until the site manager evicts them, there will be another gone from the building by four o'clock but doing just as much work at home. The work–life balance of your colleague who has young children will be very different from that of a singleton with no family commitments. Some will spend their weekends with their noses in a book, others in front of a large or small screen, and the more adventurous will be up a mountain, down a cave or in some depth of water, salty or fresh. However our colleagues choose to spend their time is up to them and not for anyone, whatever their role in the school, to judge or comment upon.

However, for our teachers and other colleagues to make this choice, wellbeing needs to be enabled, supported and sustained. It is going to look different for everyone because we are all different with a range of life experiences, values, attitudes, needs, frailties, feelings, and levels of resilience and empathy. We don't have a school full of soulless automatons; we are staffed with real authentic people, with actual emotions and real lives. If we don't give them the wherewithal to lead their lives, express their emotions and ultimately be themselves, they will be subsumed by the sheer overload of workload and pressures. Do we want our teachers to perform as people or perform as puppets?

Are we cascading the pressures from outside our schools down to our colleagues? Are the perceived or actual expectations from our local authorities, MATs, the DfE and Ofsted cranking up the pressure on our teachers or do school leaders act as the filter, or the dam, of that gravity of expectation?

On my journey through researching and writing *The Wellbeing Toolkit*, it has become increasingly apparent that this is only the very beginning of a conversation about wellbeing. As the negative experiences of teachers came into focus during my research, it became apparent as to how widespread the behaviours and attitudes that impacted upon the mental wellbeing of our staff were. However, it is also very clear that there are many excellent leaders out there who are making wellbeing a school priority for their children as well as their staff.

Wellbeing matters. It really matters. Where it is absent or neglected, dismissed or relegated down the priority scale, where wellbeing is not supported and where school cultures are at their most toxic, staff will be concerned for their job security. This in turn threatens their mental wellbeing, their relationships, their livelihood, and their capacity to pay their bills and their mortgages. If anyone plays games with the wellbeing of your teachers or support staff, they play games with the wellbeing of their spouses and partners, of their children and other loved ones. The consequences of such actions do not bear consideration. Ignore wellbeing and there's a price to pay in terms of the length of service of your staff, not only in your school but in the profession.

Achieving work–life balance may to some be a utopian ideal and, as we have seen through this book, in many cases the balance and the very notion that wellbeing can be supported is dismissed as unobtainable. As we know, there is a crisis in recruitment of teachers and in retaining them. The pool of potential headteachers is shrinking too. Budget cuts, restructuring and redundancy place all of our wellbeing under strain. The wellbeing of the teaching profession and of the support staff in our schools needs to be of paramount importance because good physical and mental wellbeing for our pupils needs to begin with the wellbeing of our adults.

We may not have the funding that we desire but we can have our principles, the very principles and values that fill our wellbeing toolkit and equip us with the desire, willingness and sheer determination to ensure that every single member of our school staff has the resilience, support and care they need to enable them to fulfil their role. Employing our core values, applying them, living and breathing them, needs authenticity of action, not empty words. Being empathetic and collaborative, supportive and celebratory, showing trust and building mutual respect all take time but are essential to the culture of a school where our teachers and teaching assistants can thrive and grow.

Consider the allegory for the human condition that is represented in L. Frank Baum's *The Wonderful Wizard of Oz* and its characters. Whilst we might think of the Wicked Witch of the West as representative of the barriers to wellbeing, it is the values and principles embodied by the Good Witch of the South and the eponymous Wizard that Dorothy learns to follow to the benefit of her new companions. Whilst Scarecrow wishes for a brain, it is the courage of the Cowardly Lion and the heart of the Tin Woodman that complete the rounded persona of Dorothy's friends. It is this same rounded persona that is demonstrated by the school leaders who utilise their wellbeing toolkit to maintain year-round concern for their staff, rather than use it solely for emergency repair. The schools with the best wellbeing should aim not merely to have a brain, but to have a heart and a soul too.

Further reading

I have drawn inspiration from the following texts in compiling this work and in defining what leading wellbeing means to me. I would recommend these sources to anyone looking for further reading items. There is a scattering of education texts, familiar to some readers, but there are also texts from a wider field, which emphasises the universality of wellbeing.

Bethune, A. (2018), *Wellbeing in the Primary Classroom: A practical guide to teaching happiness*. London: Bloomsbury Education.

Christodoulou, D. (2017), *Making Good Progress? The future of Assessment for Learning*. Oxford: Oxford University Press.

Dix, P. (2017), *When the Adults Change, Everything Changes: Seismic shifts in school behaviour*. Carmarthen: Independent Thinking Press.

Dunford, J. (2016), *The School Leadership Journey*. Woodbridge: John Catt Educational.

Ferguson, A. (2016), *Leading: Lessons in leadership from the legendary Manchester United manager*. London: Hodder and Stoughton.

Field, T. (1996), *Bully in Sight: How to predict, resist, challenge and combat workplace bullying*. Didcot: Success Unlimited.

Hawkes, N. (2013), *From My Heart: Transforming lives through values*. Carmarthen: Independent Thinking Press.

Kell, E. (2018), *How to Survive in Teaching: Without imploding, exploding or walking away*. London: Bloomsbury Education.

Myatt, M. (2016), *High Challenge, Low Threat: How the best leaders find the balance*. Woodbridge: John Catt Educational.

Nicholas, L. and West-Burnham, J. (2016), *Understanding Leadership: Challenges and reflections*. Carmarthen: Crown House.

Pye, J. (1989), *Invisible Children: Who are the real losers at school?* Oxford: Oxford University Press.

Syed, M. (2015), *Black Box Thinking: Marginal gains and the secret of high performance*. London: John Murray.

Syed, M. (2017), *The Greatest: The quest for sporting perfection*. London: John Murray.

Useful websites

Staff support and counselling

Education Support Partnership: www.educationsupportpartnership.org.uk

Parental rights

The MaternityTeacher PaternityTeacher Project: www.mtpt.org.uk

National Education Union maternity advice: www.teachers.org.uk/help-and-advice/self-help/m/maternity matters

Maternity Action UK: www.maternityaction.org.uk

Child bereavement

Child Bereavement UK: www.childbereavementuk.org/for-schools

Young Minds: www.youngminds.org.uk

Influential wellbeing tweeters

On my wellbeing journey and in compiling *The Wellbeing Toolkit* I have encountered some very dedicated people, 'Wellbeing Superheroes' as we call them at Healthy Toolkit HQ. Some of them I have had the pleasure to meet in person, which is a more meaningful interaction than the relative anonymity of Twitter. Some of these people have been on the sharp end, or the blunt end, depending how you see it, of wellbeing and workload management. Everyone on this list lives, breathes and believes in wellbeing and shares the values and principles of *The Wellbeing Toolkit* with me.

The Healthy Toolkit team

@HealthyToolkit was set up as a Twitter account and blog (https://healthyteachertoolkit.wordpress.com) in August 2016, recognising the need to address whole-school health and wellbeing issues.

@Artology – Helen Dlamini: Helen is a co-founder of @HealthyToolkit and a leader of art, PSHE and wellbeing in her MAT where she also takes a lead in supporting young people's mental health and wellbeing. Helen also tweets on the @HealthyToolkit account.

@DaringOptimist – Maria O'Neill: Maria is a co-founder of @HealthyToolkit and founder of @UKPastoralChat. Maria teaches modern foreign languages, is a wellbeing coach, specialises in digital wellbeing and e-safety, is a believer in authentic values for leadership and is an advocate for @WomenEd. Maria tweets knowledgeably and passionately on wellbeing and values issues.

@MattGovernor – Matt Young: Matt is also a co-founder of @HealthyToolkit and lead for @UKPastoralChat. As a current governor Matt is an impassioned advocate for SEND and a supporter of @BAMEedNetwork and a #HeForShe supporter of @WomenEd. Matt tweets his support for a range of key issues including teacher wellbeing, which he keenly supports in his governor role.

@anoara_a – Anoara Mughal: I first met Anoara when she accidentally found herself speaking at a WomenEd event and had to be more than ten per cent braver as a result. Now in an assistant headteacher role, Anoara tweets about great books to use in the primary classroom, as well as her dedication to wellbeing.

Great supporters of the Healthy Toolkit team

@cherrylkd: Cherryl is one of the first teachers I found on Twitter and has been a wonderful support in all that time. Cherryl is an assistant headteacher at an outstanding special school in Blackpool and my go-to authority on SEND, on which she has also written for Bloomsbury.

@jordyjax: Former deputy headteacher at a PRU and passionate about preventing exclusion.

@AdrianBethune: Teacher and author of *Wellbeing in the Primary Classroom*.

@mindworkmatters: Kelly Hannaghan leads wellbeing at Lessness Heath Primary School in Bexley.

@mindfulmiss1: Deputy headteacher in a sixth form and passionate about wellbeing and mindfulness.

@musicmind: Mental health ambassador, author and motivator.

@MrGPrimary: Primary teacher and blogger.

@MrDPortman: Learning mentor at Parklands.

@zoecaine: School governor and wellbeing advocate.

@MalCPD: Coach, consultant and leadership facilitator.

@bbcTeaching: Primary teacher and #BrewEdManchester organiser.

@MrPatelsAwesome: #HeForShe, #BAME, #MH advocate.

@JeevanSChagger: Health mentor and ambassador for @GoNoodle.

@venglishILS: Education consultant and MHFA Youth instructor.

@RaeSnape: Headteacher – likes flamingos.

@smithsmm: Headteacher and curator of picture book lists across the primary phase.

@Ed_Tmprince: Headteacher, author and mindfulness advocate.

@lisafathersAFL: Director of teaching school.

Wellbeing leaders and writers

@thosethatcan: Dr Emma Kell, author of *How to Survive in Teaching*, also available from Bloomsbury.

@lessnessheathht: Katy O'Connor is Headteacher at Lessness Heath Primary School.

@TeachersMHaW: Georgia Holleran organised the first Teach Well Fest at Passmores Academy.

@Vivgrant: Director of Integrity Coaching and wellbeing advocate.

@MrsHumanities: Victoria shares her personal tale of the other side of wellbeing through her tweets and blog.

@samschoolstuff: Sam's website is packed with simple and practical wellbeing advice.

@jstanthinks: Julian Stanley is the driving force behind the Education Support Partnership.

@MrsTweddell: Wellbeing coordinator.

@teachwellall: Steve Waters at the Teach Well Alliance.

@nourishworkplce: Kimberley Evans is dedicated to keeping teachers happy and healthy.

@maternityCPD: Emma and Charlotte empower teachers to continue their professional development whilst on parental leave and promote family-friendly school cultures.

Headteachers and school leaders who give priority to wellbeing

@MonikaKaur100: Monika Sandhu is an assistant headteacher with responsibility for staff development and wellbeing. She has a real passion for the wellbeing of her colleagues and shared her practical wellbeing strategies for *The Wellbeing Toolkit*.

@ottleyoconnor: Patrick lives the practical side of wellbeing having led several schools on an interim basis. A man who puts the love back into leadership and actively encourages his staff to make the most of their holidays, by planning these as tightly as term time.

@chrisdysonHT: Chris has his own section in the book – it is all there!

@f33lthesun: Also at Parklands 'The Lovely Beth' – and she is!

@Ethical_Leader: Hannah Wilson, Head of Aureus School and founder of WomenEd.

@lenabellina: Leading wellbeing in Scotland.

@jillberry102: Formerly a headteacher, now a leadership consultant. Very kindly agreed to write the foreword for *The Wellbeing Toolkit*.

References

BBC (2013), 'Teachers increasingly dissatisfied, survey suggests', 26th June, https://www.bbc.co.uk/news/education-23052775

Bennett, B. (2018), 'I can never thank @chrisdysonHT enough for believing in me when I didn't and saving me from myself!' (Tweet), 9th February, https://twitter.com/f33lthesun/status/962077280582299648

Bethune, A. (2018), *Wellbeing in the Primary Classroom: A practical guide to teaching happiness*. London: Bloomsbury Education.

Department for Education (2016a), 'Reducing teacher workload: Data Management Review Group report', https://www.gov.uk/government/publications/reducing-teacher-workload-data-management-review-group-report

Department for Education (2016b), 'Reducing teacher workload: Marking Policy Review Group report', https://www.gov.uk/government/publications/reducing-teacher-workload-marking-policy-review-group-report

Department for Education (2016c), 'Reducing teacher workload: Planning and Resources Group report', https://www.gov.uk/government/publications/reducing-teacher-workload-planning-and-resources-group-report

Department for Education (2017a), 'School teachers' pay and conditions', https://www.gov.uk/government/publications/school-teachers-pay-and-conditions

Department for Education (2017b), 'School workforce in England: November 2016', https://www.gov.uk/government/uploads/system/uploads/attachment_data/file/620825/SFR25_2017_MainText.pdf

Dix, P. (2017), *When the Adults Change, Everything Changes: Seismic shifts in school behaviour*. Carmarthen: Independent Thinking Press.

Education Support Partnership (2018), 'New research highlights concern about teacher wellbeing over the summer break', 26th July, https://www.educationsupportpartnership.org.uk/about-us/press-centre/new-research-highlights-concern-about-teacher-wellbeing-over-summer-break

Elliott, V., Baird, J. A., Hopfenbeck, T., Ingram, J., Thompson, I., Usher, N., Zantout, M., Richardson, J. and Coleman, R. (2016), 'A marked improvement? A review of the evidence on written marking', Education Endowment Foundation, https://educationendowmentfoundation.org.uk/public/files/Publications/EEF_Marking_Review_April_2016.pdf

Fahie, D. and Devine, D. (2014) 'The impact of workplace bullying on primary school teachers and principals', *Scandinavian Journal of Educational Research*, 58, (2), 235–252.

Fawbert, D. (2018), 'New letter reveals the 11 commandments of football management, according to Sir Bobby Robson', *Shortlist*, https://www.shortlist.com/entertainment/world-cup/bobby-robson-management-rules-gareth-southgate-england-newcastle/364130

Ferguson, A. (2016), *Leading: Lessons in leadership from the legendary Manchester United manager*. London: Hodder and Stoughton.

George, M. (2018), 'Lib Dems want to abolish Ofsted, Sats and league tables', *TES*, 5th March, https://www.tes.com/news/lib-dems-want-abolish-ofsted-sats-and-league-tables

Guardian (2006), 'David Cameron's speech to Google Zeitgeist Europe 2006', 22nd May, https://www.theguardian.com/politics/2006/may/22/conservatives.davidcameron

Hall, M. (2013), 'Teachers are the happiest workers in Britain, says survey', *Telegraph*, 29th April, https://www.telegraph.co.uk/education/educationnews/10025085/Teachers-are-the-happiest-workers-in-Britain-says-survey.html

Harford, S. (2017a), 'Okay #SLT what's one thing you'll pledge to do to reduce your teachers' workload in the coming new year?' (Tweet), 31st August, https://twitter.com/harfordsean/status/903316260158656512

Harford, S. (2017b), 'Tackling workload together – a new question for staff at the point of inspection', *Ofsted blog*, https://educationinspection.blog.gov.uk/2017/09/14/tackling-workload-together-a-new-question-for-staff-at-the-point-of-inspection/

Hazell, W. (2018), 'Cap teachers' hours and abolish Ofsted to cut workload, Hinds told', *TES*, 9th April, https://www.tes.com/news/cap-teachers-hours-and-abolish-ofsted-cut-workload-hinds-told

Leeds Beckett University (2018), 'Depression and stress commonplace amongst trainee teachers', 7th August, http://www.leedsbeckett.ac.uk/news/0818-depression-and-stress-commonplace-amongst-trainee-teachers/

Mayor of London (2017), 'The Mayor's Education Conference: Event Report 2017', https://www.london.gov.uk/sites/default/files/mayors_education_conference_-_2017_report.pdf

Mindfulness Foundation (2015), 'Policy: where the parties stand on wellbeing', https://www.mindfulnessfoundation.org.uk/campaigns/2015-election/wellbeing-policy/

Myatt, M. (2016), *High Challenge, Low Threat: How the best leaders find the balance*. Woodbridge: John Catt Educational.

National Education Union (2016), 'Education in chaos: a survey of NUT school leadership members uncovers a chorus of concern about Government education policies', https://www.teachers.org.uk/news-events/conference-2016/education-chaos-survey-leadership

National Education Union (2017), 'Teacher recruitment and retention', https://www.teachers.org.uk/edufacts/teacher-recruitment-and-retention

Office for National Statistics (2018), 'Measures of National Well-being Dashboard', https://www.ons.gov.uk/peoplepopulationandcommunity/wellbeing/articles/measuresofnationalwellbeingdashboard/2018-04-25

Ofsted (2017), 'Inspection report: Parklands Primary School, 12–13 September 2017', Crown Copyright, https://www.parklandsprimary.org.uk/wp-content/uploads/2017/10/Parklands-Primary-School-10023979-Final-Report.pdf

Ofsted (2018), 'Ofsted inspections: myths', https://www.gov.uk/government/publications/school-inspection-handbook-from-september-2015/ofsted-inspections-mythbusting

Palacio, R. J. (2013), *Wonder*. London: The Bodley Head.

Pye, J. (1989), *Invisible Children: Who are the real losers at school?* Oxford: Oxford University Press.

Roberts, J. (2018), 'Ofsted "needs a plan" to stop losing inspectors to MATs', *TES*, 24th May, https://www.tes.com/news/ofsted-needs-plan-stop-losing-inspectors-mats

SART (2018), 'National summary report', https://www.sartcorsonline.com/rptCSR_PublicMultYear.aspx?ClinicPKID=0

Scott, S. (2016), 'New findings reveal teacher training drop-out rates', *Schools Week*, 6th July, https://schoolsweek.co.uk/what-is-going-on-with-recruitment-and-retention/

Scutt, C. (2017), 'Cutting workload isn't enough to stop teachers leaving schools', *Guardian*, 16th November, https://www.theguardian.com/teacher-network/2017/nov/16/to-stop-teachers-leaving-the-profession-lets-help-them-make-a-difference

TES (2018), 'Banned: Teacher who called pupils c**** on Facebook', 17th August, https://www.tes.com/news/banned-teacher-who-called-pupils-c-facebook

Whittaker, F. (2018), 'Damian Hinds speech to NAHT conference: the full text', *Schools Week*, 4th May, https://schoolsweek.co.uk/damian-hinds-speech-to-naht-conference-the-full-text/

Index